Empower
English
Language
Learners

WITH

Tools From
the Web

This book is dedicated to my "boys": Thank you for your patience,
your inspiration, and your seemingly endless supply of hugs and kisses. Most of all,
thanks for each having your own laptop so you don't have to use mine! Los adoro . . .

Lori Langer de Ramirez

Empower English Language Learners

with

Tools From the Web

CORWIN
A SAGE Company

For information:

Corwin
A SAGE Company
2455 Teller Road
Thousand Oaks, California 91320
(800) 233-9936
Fax: (800) 417-2466
www.corwinpress.com

SAGE Ltd.
1 Oliver's Yard
55 City Road
London EC1Y 1SP
United Kingdom

SAGE Pvt. Ltd.
B 1/I 1 Mohan Cooperative
    Industrial Area
Mathura Road, New Delhi 110 044
India

SAGE Asia-Pacific Pte. Ltd.
33 Pekin Street #02-01
Far East Square
Singapore 048763

Printed in the United States of America

Library of Congress Cataloging-in-Publication Data

Langer de Ramirez, Lori.
Empower English language learners with tools from the web / Lori Langer de Ramirez.
    p. cm.
Includes bibliographical references and index.
ISBN 978-1-4129-7242-0 (cloth: alk. paper)
ISBN 978-1-4129-7243-7 (pbk.: alk. paper)
    1. English language—Study and teaching—Foreign speakers. 2. English language—Study and teaching—Technological innovations. 3. English language—Computer-assisted instruction. 4. Web-based instruction. 5. Educational technology. I. Title.

PE1128.A2L294 2010
428.0078'54678—dc22   2009036786

This book is printed on acid-free paper.

09   10   11   12   13   10 9 8 7 6 5 4 3 2 1

Acquisitions Editor:	Debra Stollenwerk
Associate Editor:	Julie McNall
Production Editor:	Veronica Stapleton
Copy Editor:	Adam Dunham
Typesetter:	C&M Digitals (P) Ltd.
Proofreader:	Dennis W. Webb
Indexer:	Sheila Bodell
Cover Designer:	Rose Storey

Contents

Preface

RATIONALE

According to Wikipedia (see Chapter 3 for a discussion of wikis and Wikipedia): "the term 'Web 2.0' is defined as World Wide Web technology and web design that enhance creativity, communications, secure information sharing, collaboration and functionality of the web" (Accessed on 1/9/2009 at http://en.wikipedia.org/wiki/Web_2.0). Web 2.0 technologies represent a shift from passive use of the Internet, where users mainly engaged in accessing information (finding and viewing, listening to or reading), to active use of the "read/write" Web in which users not only access information but also create it, upload it, and share it with others (an active-user model). This shift represents incredible opportunities for students to create work and post it to the Web for audiences beyond the walls of their classrooms and schools. These Web 2.0 tools not only have the potential to revolutionize our classrooms, they have particularly valuable uses in the teaching of English language learners.

Given that a new Web 2.0 Web site, program, or tool is developed on a weekly (perhaps daily) basis, making the possibilities seemingly endless for teaching all subject areas—especially languages—it is easy to feel overwhelmed by the sheer quantities of new sites and programs for education. Teachers often report feeling that their students are miles ahead of them—and that the gap gets wider each day.

Students come to school as *digital natives.* Today's students have grown up with computers and the Internet and are comfortable using technology for work and play. They use technology with fluency and ease. Many teachers, however, are *digital immigrants* who learned to use technology but may not be as fluent, flexible, or comfortable with it as our students are. When students come to our classrooms having chatted on Facebook or having posted and viewed YouTube videos the night before, many of us cannot relate to the role these new Web-based technologies play in their lives. It is understandable that we feel a lack of connection to these new Web sites. They seem to have a hypnotic hold on our students, and this intensity can be intimidating. But then, didn't TV have a similar effect on a previous generation of young people?

The intent of this book is three-fold: (1) to demonstrate ways in which K–12 teachers can use Web 2.0 tools with English learners to support learning; (2) to demystify some of the most popular Web sites, programs, and tools; and (3) to encourage teachers to try these tools for themselves. This book may not turn you into a digital native, but perhaps it will turn you from a struggling digital immigrant to an enthusiastic "analog expat!"

IS THIS BOOK FOR YOU?

No matter where you are on the technology continuum, this book contains suggestions, ideas, and resources for you. On a personal level, exploring Web 2.0 tools may offer you a new means of communicating with friends, sharing hobbies, or creating an online connection with groups of like-minded people. On the professional level, whether you teach elementary, middle or high school, there are activities and links provided in this book that you can use right away in your classroom. While the information in the book is targeted for use with English language learners (ELLs), you don't have to be an English as a second language (ESL) teacher to use it. Mainstream teachers with ELLs in their charge will find ample resources and suggestions for ways in which to use Web 2.0 tools with English language learners—and with all of their students. The beauty of learning about Web 2.0 tools is in their applicability to all levels of education, all subject areas, and all students. There is a tool, project, or activity on the Web ready and waiting to be tried out with all sorts of students in all sorts of schools. This book can also serve as an excellent bridge between ESL educators and subject area teachers since Web 2.0 tools facilitate cross-disciplinary collaboration. To sum up, this book is for anyone interested in learning about ways to communicate, collaborate, and celebrate via the Web and use Web 2.0 tools with their students.

HOW TO USE THIS BOOK

This book is organized by type of tool, with Chapters 2 through 4 covering one type each: blogs, wikis, and podcasts. Chapters 5 through 9 combine several different Web sites that are linked by a common usage model: viewing, creating, and sharing video (YouTube and TeacherTube), sharing visual media (Flickr and VoiceThread), social networking (Facebook and MySpace), social bookmarking (Diigo and del.icio.us), and virtual worlds (Panwapa and Teen Second Life). These divisions were designed to help teachers to think about uses of these tools in the classroom with ELLs. However, there is overlap in the ways in which many of the tools are used in the "real world." For example, Twitter can be seen as a "microblog" and Flickr is also a means of social networking. In other words, even though VoiceThread is included in this book in the chapter on sharing visual media, it does not mean that teachers and students can't use it for other purposes like connecting with another class to comment on a student's photography. After you feel comfortable with these tools, be creative and design your own uses for them.

Each chapter is organized around six central questions:

What?   *What is this tool?* What does it do? In this section, information is provided about the tool, how it works, and what the main features look like.

Why?   *Why is this tool great for ELLs?* Why should students learn to use it to create work in school? This section will provide a rationale for the benefits of the technology with English language learners.

How?   *How are teachers using this tool with ELLs?* How does a lesson using this tool work in the ESL classroom? We will explore in detail activities created by ESL teachers that are aligned to both the TESOL standards and the 21st-century skills. Finally, a short bulleted list of possible activities for each tool is provided.

When?   *When can I use this tool with my ELLs?* Expanding on the previous section, adaptations of the activities—as well as alternative activities—will be provided for teachers of students in grades K–5, 6–8, and 9–12.

Who?   *Who is using this tool with ELLs?* We will hear from an ESL teacher who has learned to love the technology covered in the chapter. In a personal narrative, the teacher shares the challenges and the successes in using the tool with ESL students.

Where?   *Where can we find more information?* To complete each chapter, there is list of links to online resources and a bibliography of further readings on the chapter topic.

There are also several special features in the book that are meant to provide you with clear examples and extra information. These include

- A video preview link: Each chapter begins with a link to a short video that introduces the tool in an informative and entertaining way. Most of these videos come from the wildly popular Common Craft series entitled "Explanations in Plain English." The entire series can be found online at http://www.commoncraft.com/. Aside from explanations of Web 2.0 tools, try the excellent "Electing a U.S. President in Plain English," (http://www.commoncraft.com/election) or the highly entertaining: "Zombies in Plain English"! (http://www.common craft.com/zombies).
- Screenshots: There are many annotated screenshots (pictures of a computer screen) in this book. They are there to help highlight a special feature or aspect of a particular Web 2.0 tool. They are also meant to show you a preview of what you can expect online once you dive into using a tool for your own personal or school use. Please note that since the World Wide Web is a fluid and everchanging medium, many of the screenshots that you see in the book will have changed over time. For instance, the homepage of PodOMatic

(a podcasting Web site) or Blogger (a blogging tool) may look slightly different from the one you see in the screenshot in this book. Don't panic! The essential features will all be there—it might just mean that you will have to search for them a little. Overall, though, the screenshots should give you the taste and feel for the Web 2.0 tools you plan to explore.

- Student and teacher work samples: Some of the chapters feature examples of student work and/or examples of actual lesson plans that use Web 2.0 tools. These will hopefully inspire you to envision ways that that the tool might work with your own students and within your own lesson planning.

- Guidelines: Each chapter features some guidelines or suggestions for safe and appropriate use of the Web 2.0 tool with students. Some of these guidelines focus on the creation of a quality project (and thus deal with form), while others are suggestions for protecting students' identities and safety while online (a focus on process). These guidelines are no substitute for your own set of rules and regulations that are tailored to your school context, but they *are* teacher tested and parent approved, and they can serve as the building blocks for your own guidelines.

- Quick lists: These are short bulleted lists of ways you might use a particular Web 2.0 tool. These lists are quick glimpses of the ways that others have already discovered to make use of Web 2.0 tools with students. They are not exhaustive, however. You can view them as the start of a brainstorm about ways to use a tool—try to see how many more uses you can add!

ONE FINAL NOTE

The aim of this book is to provide teachers on all ends of the spectrum—between "technophobe" and "technophile"—with enough information to raise comfort levels, or entice more savvy users, to put down the book at any given moment, dive into a particular tool or Web site, and plan something for their ELLs for the next school day. To this end, it is hoped that this book will serve as a gentle mentor to sit beside teachers as these tools are explored. It is also helpful to find a real life mentor—someone who is helpful, knowledgeable, comforting, and encouraging. Either way, jump in to the world of Web 2.0 tools—the water's fine!

Acknowledgments

There are many talented, creative, and dedicated teachers, staff developers, administrators, professors, and students working with Web 2.0 tools on the World Wide Web. I have been consistently thrilled with the generosity of these educators—and impressed by the speed with which people answered my e-mail requests for permissions. In the process of researching and writing this book, I have come across hundreds of project lessons, checklists, guidelines, and activity suggestions posted on blogs, wikis, and Web sites sponsored by these educators—and many of them appear as models in this book. I thank and tip my hat to the following professionals and colleagues who have contributed material to this book: Sean Banville, Jed Chan, Ellen Clegg, Anne Collier, Anne P. Davis, Larry Ferlazzo, Wes Fryer, Amie Garnache, Valerie Gee, Gabriela Grosseck, Miguel Guehlin, Jeanne Halderson, Carmen Holotescu, Matt Horne, Charles Kelly, Ronaldo Lima, Steve McCrea, Kathleen Mitchell, Nik Peachey, Elizabeth Ramsay, and Heather Tatton.

Special thanks to my editor, Debbie Stollenwerk, who is unfailingly helpful, enthusiastic, insightful, and just plain fun to work with; to editor Julie McNall for always being just a click away with excellent suggestions and help; and to my very brilliant Yalie nephew, George Norberg, for his permissions assistance and insightful feedback on the manuscript.

Believe it or not, I started my teaching career as a technophobe. But, I was lucky enough to receive help and support from colleague and friend Neale McGoldrick, currently chair of the history department at SMIC School in Shanghai, China, where she teaches history and also Photoshop. Years ago at a school in New York City, Neale sat next to me, eased my anxieties, inspired my creativity, and taught me to love the computer for all it offered to me and my students. It is my hope that all educators who read this book can also count on a gentle mentor—a flesh-and-blood colleague-friend—who can help, inspire, and guide them in their exploration of Web 2.0 tools.

Corwin wishes to acknowledge the following peer reviewers for their editorial insight and guidance.

Holly Hansen-Thomas, Ph.D.
Assistant Professor of Bilingual and ESL Education
Texas Woman's University
Denton, TX

Denise Lewis Harlos, Ed. S.
Educational Program Development
Shakopee Public Schools
Shakopee, MN

Jacie Maslyk
Elementary Principal
Carlynton School District
Pittsburgh, PA

Victoria Pilotti
Adjunct
St. John's University, Graduate School of Education,
    TESOL Department
Queens, NY

About the Author

 **Lori Langer de Ramirez** began her career as a teacher of Spanish, French, and ESL. She holds a master's degree in applied linguistics and a doctorate in curriculum and teaching from Teachers College, Columbia University. She is currently the Chairperson of the ESL and World Language Department for Herricks Public Schools.

Lori is the author of *Take Action: Lesson Plans for the Multicultural Classroom* and *Voices of Diversity: Stories, Activities and Resources for the Multicultural Classroom* (Pearson), as well as several Spanish-language books and texts (*Cuéntame—Folklore y Fábulas* and *Mi abuela ya no está*). She has contributed to many textbooks and written numerous articles about second-language pedagogy and methodology. Her interactive Web site (www.miscositas.com) offers teachers over 40 virtual picture books, videos, wiki and blog links, and other curricular materials for teaching Chinese, English, French, Indonesian, Italian, Spanish, and Thai.

In the past decade, Lori has presented over 50 workshops, staff development trainings, and addresses at local, regional, and national conferences and in schools throughout the United States (Connecticut, Illinois, Iowa, Massachusetts, New Jersey, New Mexico, New York, Pennsylvania, Tennessee, Texas, Virginia, and Washington, D.C.) and abroad (the Dominican Republic, Germany, Puerto Rico, Thailand, and Venezuela).

She is the recipient of the Nelson Brooks Award for Excellence in the Teaching of Culture, several National Endowment for the Humanities grants for study in Mexico, Colombia, and Senegal, and a Fulbright Award to India and Nepal. Her areas of research and curriculum development are multicultural and diversity education, folktales in the language classroom, and technology in language teaching.

Why Use Web 2.0 Tools With ELLs?

INTRODUCTION

Web 2.0 tools are becoming more and more commonplace in schools. With the change of a "read" Web to a "read/write" Web, teachers are discovering new ways in which to engage technologically savvy students in computer-based educational activities. Publishing student work to the World Wide Web is a means of providing an authentic global audience for classroom productions. When students write or speak for a broader and more international audience, they pay more attention to polishing their work, think more deeply about the content they produce, and consider cultural norms more thoughtfully. These benefits serve to strengthen all students' skills, but they are particularly relevant to the English language learner (ELL) who is beginning to acquire or continuing to develop his or her proficiency in English in the school setting.

ELL'S IN SCHOOLS: SOME CHALLENGES TO CONSIDER

According to the National Clearinghouse for English Language Acquisition and Language Instruction Educational Programs (n.d.):

> Based on state-reported data, it is estimated that 5,119,561 ELL students were enrolled in public schools (pre–K through Grade 12) for the 2004–2005 school year. This number represents approximately

10.5% of total public school student enrollment, and a 56.2% increase over the reported 1994–95 total public school ELL enrollment. Among the states, California enrolled the largest number of public school ELL students, with 1,591,525, followed by Texas (684,007), Florida (299,346), New York (203,583), Illinois (192,764), and Arizona (155,789).

Whether you are an ESL teacher or a teacher of any other subject area, you have almost definitely worked with English language learners in your classrooms. These eager students are faced with the challenge of learning a new language and culture while also studying subjects like science, math, English language arts, art, music, physical education, and health. This can be an incredibly daunting task—even for the strongest of students who have consistent schooling and can demonstrate good literacy in their first language.

According to educational researcher Jim Cummins (1979), English language learners acquire basic interpersonal communicative skills (BICS)—also known as *social language*—within the first two years of exposure to English. This is the language of personal conversations, expressing opinions, requests for information, and expressions of need. However, it takes between five and seven years to develop their cognitive academic language proficiency (CALP)—also known as *academic language*. CALP is the language of textbooks, class lectures, essays, and educational videos. It is the language that students need to succeed in their academic life in an English language medium school (Cummins, 1979).

When thinking about BICS and CALP, it can be enlightening to consider a hypothetical situation in which you were a teenager and somehow relocated to the Philippines to attend a public school there. You will likely learn key words and phrases in Tagalog fairly quickly. It will take a lot longer to be able to write a cohesive essay on the history of the Philippine rainforest—*in Tagalog* (note: for a more challenging scenario, replace the Philippines with Thailand, where not only the language is different, but so is the script).

So, time is of the essence, and yet our ELLs can't afford to wait on either front. They must learn English alongside their other subjects. They don't have the luxury of acquiring CALP first and then entering classes involving the other disciplines. The challenge to learn English and succeed in school—not successively but rather simultaneously—is a daunting one, but it is quite common in most schools across the United States.

WHY WEB 2.0 WITH ELL'S?

The gift of time is the greatest gift that an ELL could possibly receive in school. But since the gift of time is one that we simply cannot give, we must look for ways to extend English language acquisition beyond the school day and means of maximizing learning for our students. Web 2.0

tools can provide students with extra opportunities to do meaningful language-learning tasks from the comforts of their own homes or local libraries. On a receptive level, they can sign on to a podcast for extra listening practice or view an instructive video on YouTube. However, Web 2.0 tools work best when students are asked to develop, create, and share their work online. It is in this way that they are active learners, negotiating meaning and creating media for a worldwide audience. For example, students can "meet" virtually with classmates via the Web and work on collaborative projects on a wiki. They can also create blog entries, videos, or comment on a classmate's work—all after the school building has closed down for the day.

For beginning English language learners in particular, Web-based platforms can also provide a safer, more anonymous space in which to practice English. Beginners can be reticent and uncomfortable speaking in class, sharing their writing with peers in a face-to-face situation, or presenting work to large groups. Part of the reluctance comes from insecurity and fear of making errors and often coincides with the "silent period" in which students are taking in the new language but not yet ready to start producing it on their own. Web 2.0 tools are particularly helpful during these early stages of acquisition as they allow ELLs to be in control by giving them the opportunity to produce work in a controlled setting. If they are creating videos or audio files, they can practice, record, and rerecord until they are satisfied with their work. If using a wiki, they can cocreate work with the help of a stronger peer in a comfortable, nonthreatening online environment. Virtual worlds like Teen Second Life offer students an anonymous place in which to meet others, have conversations, and make mistakes—without need to do so in person. Web 2.0 tools are forgiving of errors and provide students with ways to save face as they practice their new language in cyberspace.

Web 2.0 tools are also beneficial in that they support and even entice students to become creators and not merely recipients of knowledge. According to the Partnership for 21st Century Skills, it is crucial that our students come away from their K–12 educational experience with the ability to not just consume information but also create it. This creation of information has gone from a one-person endeavor to a collaboration with people from many different cultures and from all parts of the world.

Using Web 2.0 tools in the classroom involves students in activities that expand their problem-solving skills as they are required not just to find information but also to judge its worth and accuracy. With the inception of the read-write Web, anyone is capable of authoring material. This democratization of the Web has lead to a proliferation of information—not all of it trustworthy. Media literacy—in the past mainly focused on television and print media—now includes the Web and its explosion of information and material. And since ELLs are only just acquiring more challenging language, such as idiomatic expressions, they are especially vulnerable to advertisements and other media that often use this type of language as a means of persuading audiences. Now more than ever, it is imperative that our students become critical consumers of the material that is available to them at the click of a computer key.

While there are many reasons why Web 2.0 tools are beneficial for ELLs, perhaps the most convincing reason is the one that we teachers often underestimate: The World Wide Web is fun! There is a solid base of research available on the link between the use of technology with English language learners and motivation and/or improvement in certain skill areas. A study by Johns and Tórrez in 2001 found that "the new technologies offer many possibilities to the second language learner" (p. 11). Svedkauskaite, Reza-Hernandez, and Clifford (2003) have also found that

> technology has evolved from its support function to play a role in initiating learning processes. It can provide a flexible learning environment where students can really explore and be engaged. Hypermedia, for example, individually addresses levels of fluency, content knowledge, student motivation, and interest, allowing inclusion of LEP [limited English proficient] students, who can thus monitor their comprehension, language production, and behavior. ("Frameworks for Successful LEP Learners" section, para. 4)

More recently, research about the use of Web 2.0 tools in the language classroom has shown that the use of technology is appreciated by students (Stanley, 2006), linked to greater motivation (Goodwin-Jones, 2005), and tools like blogs have been responsible for improvements in students' writing (Thorne & Payne, 2005).

Students come to us with preestablished positive relationships to these technologies. They own and view MySpace and Facebook accounts, write and read blogs, create and view videos on YouTube, and record and listen to podcasts. The exciting aspect of their familiarity with these platforms is that they not only access and consume but also develop, edit, and share their work with classmates and others via the Web—and they are not being asked to do it! What better way to motivate, excite, and connect to our students than to dive into the media that they already know and love?

PREPARING ELL'S FOR THE 21ST CENTURY

English language learners in K–12 schools are charged with the task not only of acquiring a new language and increasingly challenging subject area content (i.e., science, math, social studies) but also to be a successful citizen of 21st-century global society; students are also required to be fluent in the use of the most important technologies. While it is still important to have basic core knowledge and skills in a variety of subject areas as in the past, it is no longer enough. According to theorists such as Daniel Pink (2006) and organizations like the Partnership for 21st Century Skills, students need to develop additional skills like crosscultural communication, critical thinking, and creativity and innovation skills as well. The Partnership for

21st Century Skills (www.21stcenturyskills.org) is the leading advocacy organization focused on infusing these newly important skills into education. The organization brings together the business community, education leaders, and policy makers to define a powerful vision for 21st-century education to ensure every child's success as citizens and workers in the 21st century by providing tools and resources to help facilitate and drive change. The Partnership for 21st Century Skills represents these skills through a rainbow image with the important skills listed in the rainbow and the support systems represented as pools below:

Figure 1.1

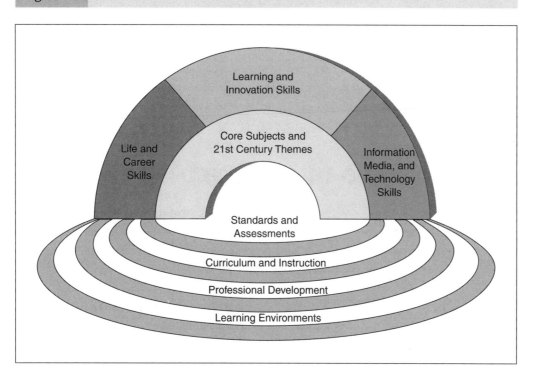

Source: Used with permission from the Partnership for 21st Century Skills.

The skills that make up that rainbow portion of the image are

1. Core Subjects and 21st-Century Themes

2. Learning and Innovation Skills:
   - Creativity and Innovation Skills
   - Critical Thinking and Problem-Solving Skills
   - Communication and Collaboration Skills

3. Information, Media, and Technology Skills:
   - Information Literacy
   - Media Literacy
   - ICT Literacy

4. Life and Career Skills:
   - Flexibility and Adaptability
   - Initiative and Self-Direction
   - Social and Cross-Cultural Skills
   - Productivity and Accountability
   - Leadership and Responsibility

Source: Used with permission from the Partnership for 21st Century Skills.

Aside from the obvious connections to information, media, and technology skills, Web 2.0 tools provide students with real opportunities to *communicate and collaborate* (Skill 2) in unique ways. Wikis, for example, foster student *creativity and innovation* (Skill 3) by allowing students to make meaning in a multimedia format. Students not only use the written word but also audio, video, and images in their own creative ways. Wikis also offer students a platform through which to coauthor articles or essays, do peer editing of projects and reports, and communicate their ideas to a wider audience. They certainly help students to show *initiative and self-direction* (Skill 4) as they design, edit, and build their wiki to best reflect their own spin on any given topic.

WEB 2.0 AND THE TESOL STANDARDS

Web 2.0 tools can also connect directly and deeply to the TESOL (Teachers of English to Speakers of Other Languages) national standards. Below is a list of the national TESOL standards, followed by examples of Web 2.0 tools and activities that correspond to each one.

Goal 1, Standard 1
To use English to communicate in social settings: Students will use English to participate in social interactions.

Example: *Blogging to share information about favorite music, families, interests*

Goal 1, Standard 2
To use English to communicate in social settings: Students will interact in, through, and with spoken and written English for personal expression and enjoyment.

Example: *Posting information about themselves in Facebook or MySpace accounts*

Goal 1, Standard 3
To use English to communicate in social settings: Students will use learning strategies to extend their communicative competence.

Example: *Commenting on friends' photos on VoiceThread or on blogs*

Goal 2, Standard 1
To use English to achieve academically in all content areas: Students will use English to interact in the classroom.

Example: *Creating a class/group podcast on a particular content area topic*

Goal 2, Standard 2	To use English to achieve academically in all content areas: Students will use English to obtain, process, construct, and provide subject matter information in spoken and written form.

Example: *Researching a topic and sharing relevant Web sites on a social bookmarking site*

Goal 2, Standard 3	To use English to achieve academically in all content areas: Students will use appropriate learning strategies to construct and apply academic knowledge.

Example: *Cocreating a group wiki on a particular content area topic*

Goal 3, Standard 1	To use English in socially and culturally appropriate ways: Students will use the appropriate language variety, register, and genre according to audience, purpose, and setting.

Example: *Creating a podcast to be broadcast on school radio or posted to the school Web site*

Goal 3, Standard 2	To use English in socially and culturally appropriate ways: Students will use nonverbal communication appropriate to audience, purpose, and setting.

Example: *Filming a video for posting to YouTube or to show in school*

Goal 3, Standard 3	To use English in socially and culturally appropriate ways: Students will use appropriate learning strategies to extend their sociolinguistic and sociocultural competence.

Example: *Sharing comments on a blog or wiki, adding comments to a photo on VoiceThread*

Source: Adapted from Teachers of English to Speakers of Other Languages (2006).

TESOL has also developed technology standards—both for students and for teachers. The technology standards for students are listed below, along with examples of student work or projects that connect to each one.

Goal 1: Language learners demonstrate foundational knowledge and skills in technology for a multilingual world

Standard 1	Language learners demonstrate basic operational skills in using various technological tools and Internet browsers.

Example: *Using Microsoft Word to write essays, Microsoft Publisher to create a brochure or book, Microsoft Excel to organize and analyze data, or Google to find information*

Standard 2	Language learners are able to use available input and output devices (e.g., keyboard, mouse, printer, headset, microphone, media player, electronic whiteboard).

Example: *Using headsets and microphones to record newscasts and to create podcasts, printing work, creating student presentations on interactive electronic whiteboards*

Standard 3   Language learners exercise appropriate caution when using online sources and when engaging in electronic communication.

Example: *Brainstorming and developing classroom guidelines for safe use of Web 2.0 tools, keeping personal information safe while sending e-mails*

Standard 4   Language learners demonstrate basic competence as users of technology.

Example: *Knowing how to find information on Google or answers to questions on WikiHow*

Goal 2: Language learners use technology in socially and culturally appropriate, legal, and ethical ways

Standard 1   Language learners understand that communication conventions differ across cultures, communities, and contexts.

Example: *Comparing and contrasting texting language from different parts of the world, using Skype to understand different cultural gestures and greetings*

Standard 2   Language learners demonstrate respect for others in their use of private and public information.

Example: *Developing Voki avatars to serve as virtual identities, not revealing addresses or other sensitive private information in e-mails or on Facebook*

Goal 3: Language learners effectively use and critically evaluate technology-based tools as aids in the development of their language-learning competence as part of formal instruction and for further learning

Standard 1   Language learners effectively use and evaluate available technology-based productivity tools.

Example: *Using Microsoft Word to write prose or poetry, using Excel for spreadsheets, posting files to GoogleDocs, finding and saving bookmarks on Diigo*

Standard 2   Language learners appropriately use and evaluate available technology-based language skill-building tools.

Example: *Using podcasts like EnglishPod to practice pronunciation, watching videos on YouTube to observe nonverbal communication*

Standard 3	Language learners appropriately use and evaluate available technology-based tools for communication and collaboration.

Example: *Using wikis to do group projects, posting comments on blogs, Skyping with classmates to practice for a class presentation*

Standard 4	Language learners use and evaluate available technology-based research tools appropriately.

Example: *Using Wikipedia to find intial information on a topic, vetting websites to determine validity*

Standard 5	Language learners recognize the value of technology to support autonomy, lifelong learning, creativity, metacognition, collaboration, personal pursuits, and productivity.

Example: *Using a variety of Web 2.0 tools to create and share school and personal information*

Source: Adapted from Teachers of English to Speakers of Other Languages (1996–2007).

The integration of Web 2.0 tools into ESL and mainstream curricula will create natural connections to these TESOL technology standards both for the students and for ESL teachers. Web 2.0 tools can help teachers develop and maintain technological skills while also learning ways to enhance student learning. These tools also allow teachers to provide more frequent and meaningful feedback and assessments while facilitating record keeping and communication with students.

SAFETY CONCERNS AND THE WEB

Before completing our discussion of the reasons for using Web 2.0 tools with our English language learners, we should address one of the biggest challenges to incorporating them into the school curriculum: safety concerns. There are legitimate fears regarding the sharing of students' identities and the posting of personal information online. However, fears based on sensationalized media reports of cyber stalkers and other relatively rare incidents can cause a school to close itself off to the powerful potential of Web 2.0 tools. According to the Web site ConnectSafely.org, some of the negative effects of "technopanics" are damaging because they

- Cause schools to fear and block digital media when they need to be teaching constructive use, employing social-technology devices, and teaching new media literacy and citizenship throughout the curriculum.
- Turn schools into barriers rather than contributors to young people's constructive use of technology.

- Increase the irrelevancy of school to active young social-technology users via the sequestering or banning of educational technology and hamstringing some of the most spirited and innovative educators.
- Reduce the competitiveness of U.S. education among developed countries already effectively employing educational technology and social media in schools.
- Reduce the competitiveness of U.S. technology and media businesses practicing good corporate citizenship where youth online safety is concerned.
- Widen the participation gap for youth—technopanics are barriers, for children and teens, to full, constructive participation in participatory culture and democracy. (Adapted from Collier, n.d.)

Every school district must come to some consensus regarding students' (and teachers') use of the Internet relating to schoolwork. Most school districts, for example, have a policy that details what can be uploaded to the school Web site, what student information can be shared online, and how students can use the Internet during the school day and for homework. Check with your school's technology specialist for information about your school's policies.

Whatever your school's rules and regulations regarding the appropriate use of Web 2.0 tools, there are ways to make the experience safe and enjoyable for your students. For example, some schools choose to allow students to post only their first names and first initial of their last names on their blogs or wikis. Other schools post video and photos of students with no names listed at all. Many schools block sites like YouTube, since students can come across inappropriate videos very easily, while others opt for allowing YouTube and teaching students how to navigate the site safely. Different rules work for different contexts. Before working with Web 2.0 tools with your students, it is important to understand your school's policies. If your school doesn't have a policy in place, volunteer to be on a committee to establish them. (Check out discussions on the topic of "Acceptable Use Policies" on the Classroom 2.0 Web site at http://www.classroom20.com/forum/topic/listForTag?tag=aup.) To help start the discussion, each chapter of this book contains a section including guidelines for safe use of a variety of Web 2.0 tools.

As the use of these technologies grows in the K–12 school setting, it is imperative that schools establish a clear and comprehensive set of rules that allow teachers and students to feel comfortable and supported in the work they do on the World Wide Web. For more detailed information, download and read the excellent publication: "Enhancing Child Safety and Online Technologies," the final report of the Internet Safety Technical Task Force to the Multi-State Working Group on Social Networking of State Attorneys General of the United States (available online at: http://cyber.law.harvard.edu/pubrelease/isttf/).

REFERENCES

Collier, A. (n.d.). Why technopanics are bad. *ConnectSafely.* Retrieved August 12, 2009, from http://www.connectsafely.org/Commentaries-Staff/why-technopanics-are-bad.html

Cummins, J. (1979). Cognitive/academic language proficiency, linguistic interdependence, the optimum age question and some other matters. *Working Papers on Bilingualism, 19,* 121–129.

Goodwin-Jones, R. (2005). Emerging technologies: Skype and podcasting: Disruptive technologies for language learning. *Language Learning and Technology, 9*(3), 9–12.

Johns, K. M., & Tórrez, N. M. (2001). Helping ESL learners succeed. *Phi Delta Kappa, 484,* 7–49.

National Clearinghouse for English Language Acquisition and Language Instruction Educational Programs, U.S. Department of Educaiton. (n.d.). *Frequently asked questions.* Retrieved August 11, 2009, from http://www.ncela.gwu.edu/faqs/

The Partnership for 21st Century Skills. (2004). *Framework for 21st century learning.* Retrieved August 12, 2009, from http://www.21stcenturyskills.org/index.php?option=com_content&task=view&id=254&Itemid=120

Pink, D. (2006). *A whole new mind.* New York: Riverhead Trade.

Stanley, G. (2006). Podcasting: Audio on the Internet comes of age. *TESL-EJ, 9*(4). Retrieved August 21, 2009, from http://www-writing.berkeley.edu/TESL-EJ/ej36/int.html

Svedkauskaite, A., Reza-Hernandez, L., & Clifford, M. (2003, June 24). *Critical issue: Using technology to support limited-English-proficient (LEP) students' learning experiences.* North Central Regional Education Laboratory. Retrieved August 11, 2009, from http://www.ncrel.org/sdrs/areas/issues/methods/technlgy/te900.htm

Teachers of English to Speakers of Other Languages. (2006). *PreK–12 English language proficiency standards.* Alexandria, VA: Author.

Teachers of English to Speakers of Other Languages. (1996–2007). *Technology standards for language learners.* Alexandria, VA: Author. Retrieved August 21, 2009, from http://www.tesol.org/s_tesol/sec_document.asp?CID=1972&DID=12051

Thorne, S., & Payne, J. (2005). Evolutionary trajectories, Internet mediated expression, and language education. *CALICO, 22*(3), 371–397.

SUGGESTED READINGS

Blake, R. J., (2008). *Brave new digital classroom: Technology and foreign language learning.* Washington, DC: Georgetown University Press.

Dudeney, G. (2007). *The Internet and the language classroom (Cambridge handbooks for language teachers).* NY: Cambridge University Press.

Green, T. D., Brown, A. H., & Robinson, L. K. (Eds.). (2007). *Making the most of the Web in your classroom: A teacher's guide to blogs, podcasts, wikis, pages, and sites.* Thousand Oaks, CA: Corwin Press.

Leu, D. J., Diadiun Leu, D., & Coiro, J. (2004). *Teaching with the Internet K–12: New literacies for new times.* Norwood, MA: Christopher Gordon.

November, A. (2001). *Empowering students with technology.* Thousand Oaks, CA: Corwin Press.

November, A. (2008). *Web literacy for educators.* Thousand Oaks, CA: Corwin Press.

Pitler, H., Hubbell, E. R., Kuhn, M., & Malenoski, K. (2007). *Using technology with classroom instruction that works.* Alexandria, VA: Association for Supervision and Curriculum Development.

Ramirez, R., Freeman, Y. S., & Freeman, D. E., (2008). *Diverse learners in the main-stream classroom: Strategies for supporting ALL students across content areas— English language learners, students with disabilities, gifted/talented students.* Portsmouth, NH: Heinemann.

Solomon, G., & Schrum, L. (2007). *Web 2.0: New tools, new schools.* Eugene, OR: International Society for Technology in Education.

HELPFUL WEB SITES

Classroom 2.0: http://www.classroom20.com

Connect Safely.org—a forum for parents, teens, experts to discuss safe socializing on the fixed and mobile Web: www.connectsafely.org

EFL and Web 2.0—an excellent online college course on a wiki page designed to teach EFL and ESL students the basics of using different Web 2.0 technologies: http://eflcourse.wikispaces.com

IALLT (International Association for Language Learning Technology): http://iallt.org

Integrating Technology Into the ESL/EFL Classroom—a series of lesson ideas with links to videos: http://integrate-technology.learnhub.com/lessons

International Society for Technology in Education: http://www.iste.org

Langwitches—a helpful blog with links and tutorials for teaching languages through technology: http://langwitches.org/blog

NCELA (National Clearinghouse for English Language Acquisition and Language Instruction Educational Programs): http://www.ncela.gwu.edu

SafeKids.com—Internet safety and civility for kids and parents: http://www.safekids.com

Social Networks and the Web 2.0 Revolution (blog post and video): http://www.teachingenglish.org.uk/blogs/nik-peachey/social-networks-web-20-revolution

2

Blogs

Online Language Portfolios

Video connection: Prior to reading this chapter, view the online video "Blogs in Plain English" at http://www.commoncraft.com/blogs

WHAT IS A BLOG?

A blog means different things to different people. Officially, the word *blog* comes from a blending of two words: Web + log = Weblog (which eventually got shortened to blog). Originally, these were Web pages on which a user could easily keep a log of Web sites that were of interest. Over time, these lists of links grew to include audio and video clips and any other information that the creator might want to include. It is an ideal space for posting thoughts and sharing ideas with others where you are likely to experience the added perk of receiving comments, feedback, support, and maybe even kudos from a community of readers.

In recent times, blogs are most commonly thought of as a means of expressing opinions about politics or other current events. Newscasters make references to blogs on the nightly news, sometimes quoting pundits from the blogosphere (the world of blogs). Candidates in political elections take the blogosphere very seriously and often have their own blogs on their official Web sites. There have even been debates over whether or not to give some of the more famous bloggers press privileges at key political events—the question being: Are these bloggers journalists, or just people like you and me who happen to comment on politics? The answer is probably *both.*

Blogs are not just for politics and pundits. People from all over the world, all age groups, with all kinds of unique interests can (and do) create blogs. Some blogs are very popular and consulted with equal respect and trust as some of the more traditional news sources, while others are more entertaining and personal. Teachers can find blogs on every topic ranging from algebra (see how educators in Texas prepare students for the Texas Assessment of Knowledge and Skills in Algebra—http://www.taksalgebra.blogspot.com/) to zoology (teacher Barry Rossheim has an interesting zoology blog at http://rossheimb.edublogs.org/). A good way to begin exploring the world of blogs is to find one that interests you and to start reading. Chances are, there is a blog (or blogs) just for you.

Components of a Blog

Once you get to a blog you'd like to investigate, what do you do? Where do you go? A blog is really a lot like other Web pages in that there is text—some of which is hyperlinked (often underlined and in blue, these links take you to another place on the page, or another page entirely). There might also images and possibly sound (like podcasts) or video on

Figure 2.1

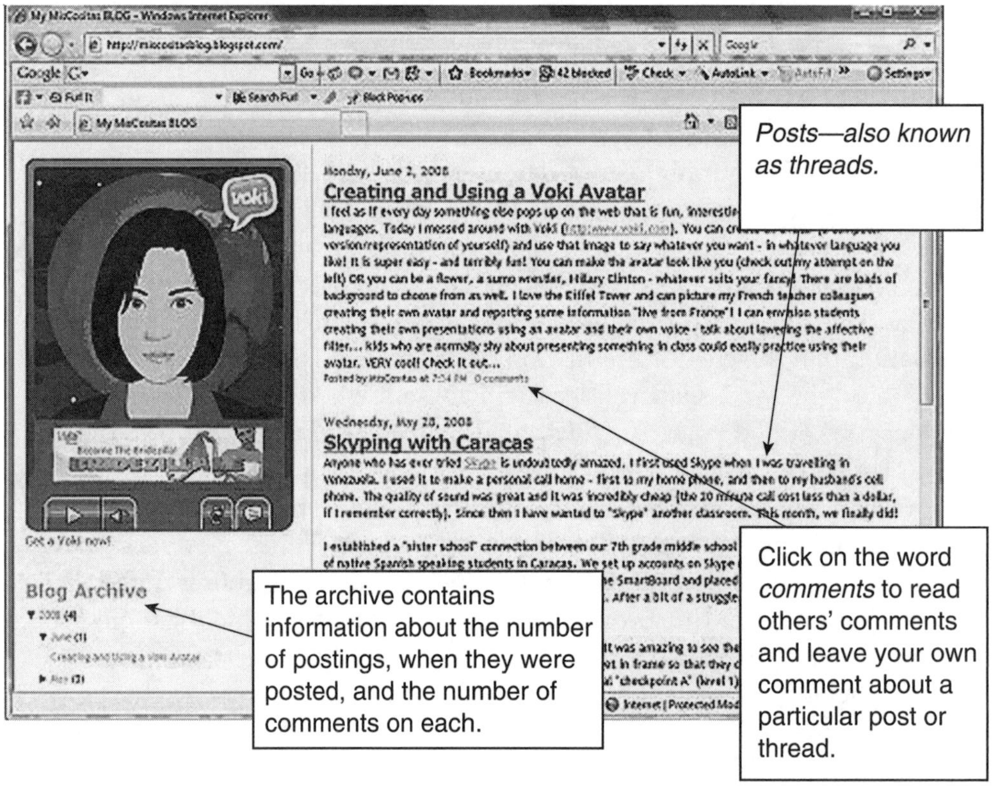
Creating and Using a Voki Avatar
Skyping with Caracas
Blog Archive
Posts—also known as threads.
The archive contains information about the number of postings, when they were posted, and the number of comments on each.
Click on the word comments to read others' comments and leave your own comment about a particular post or thread.

blogs. But there are some elements of a blog that are unique. Look at the image below for some of the typical components of a blog.

- **Post/thread:** This is the "meat" of a blog. In this section, the author of a blog posts her or his main thoughts on a topic. It may contain links within the text or even video clips.
- **Comment:** Comments can be displayed right after the original post, or they can be housed on another page. They often display the time and date the comment was posted and the screen name, user ID, or possibly e-mail address of the commentor.
- **Profile:** Often contains information about the blog's creator, such as an e-mail address, professional or educational affiliation, a list of personal interests, or even a photo (or, as in the previous sample blog, an avatar—a cartoon version of the author).
- **Links:** In a sidebar or side column, some bloggers like to include a list of links to great Web sites or to other blogs that they read regularly. This is a way of spreading the word about great blogs that people enjoy reading. The idea is that if you really like one person's blog, you will most likely appreciate what that person enjoys reading as well.
- **Archive:** As blogs gets bigger and contain more posts, an archive is useful so that people can go back and read posts from the past. Archives are often arranged by month and year. They can also be arranged by topic.

Commenting on Blogs

A great deal of the fun of blogs is posting your own comments to continue the "thread" (a term used the way we might follow the thread of a conversation) on a blog. The creator of each blog decides whether or not to allow comments on the site. Most blog sites allow bloggers to choose among the following settings (these terms are specifically from Blogger—Google's blog site, but other sites use similar terminology):

📄 **WHO CAN COMMENT?**

🖱 Anyone—includes anonymous users

🖱 Registered users—includes OpenID

🖱 Users with Google accounts

🖱 Only members of this blog

Figure 2.2

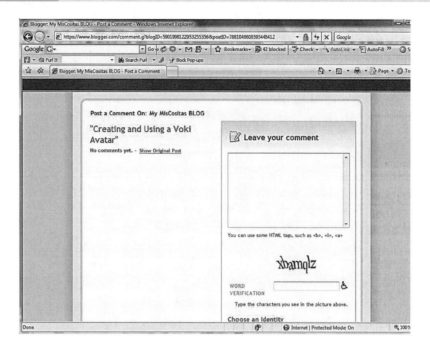

Each blog creator determines how public or private a site will be. Most blog sites allow for free commenting as reading what other people think of your posts constitutes a lot of the fun of blogging! To post, you would look for the word *comments* and click on it to leave your own thoughts:

It can get even more exciting when other visitors to a blog read not just the blogs, but your comments on the blog, and then add a comment about both! Again, the term *thread* is a propos here because a list of comments can continue the thread of the virtual conversation for as long as there is interest!

WHY READ AND WRITE BLOGS WITH ELL'S?

Blogs are particularly well suited for English language learners for a variety of reasons, motivation being one of them. Motivation in students is a topic that has been well researched. One of the main psychological theories of motivation is the "self-determination theory." It centers on three categories of needs (Deci & Ryan, 1985):

1. A sense of competence (understanding how to, and believing that one can, achieve various outcomes)

2. Relatedness to others (developing satisfactory connections to others in one's social group)

3. Autonomy (initiating and regulating one's own actions)

Blogs meet these needs for students in giving them a sense of competence in both writing and publishing (posting) their work to the Web. Students feel a connection to a broad audience of readers—and subsequently writers who may post comments to their blogs. And finally, there is a strong sense of autonomy in blogging as students may work on their own time and in their own setting in creating a blog that is personal and yet connected to a school-initiated task. This is writing with a purpose and for a real audience—and the motivational factor makes all the difference in getting ELLs to write . . . and write some more.

Having students read blogs on a variety of topics is a good place to start. As with any good genre study, the study of blogs might begin with students defining the different elements of a blog, commenting on other people's blogs, and even reviewing and giving opinions about blogs they have read.

After students have had the opportunity to read blogs, the next logical step for many teachers is to inspire students to write a blog of their own (see the "Make Your Own Blog" section later in this chapter for more details on setting up a blog for yourself or your classes). Blogs are a new way of journaling, and they can be a fun and a rewarding activity for students. And along with the satisfaction students may feel from sharing thoughts and information, they may receive comments from people who live in their own town or others who read their blogs from half way around the globe.

When a newcomer student joins a class, that student can easily be intimidated and feel too shy to express opinions freely. There is often a "silent period" in ESL students of all ages that can last anywhere from a few days to months as the student gets acclimated to a new school, a new language, and new cultures, including the school culture and the cultures of a new town, a new state, or a new country. In using blogs, ELLs are able to make comments on other students' blogs while receiving comments about their own writing. This type of communication helps the student to feel connected without forcing him to speak in class. Blogs allow often-reticent English language learners to have a voice and share ideas freely without having to speak face to face with their classmates during this challenging time.

Blogs also provide ELLs with the opportunity for their language to be read or listened to by a broad audience beyond that of their teacher and classmates. Much attention has been paid over the years of the importance of audience in writing everything from essays to research papers in the

K–12 setting. Too often, we ask students to write simply for the sake of practicing writing or to yield a grade for a particular class. Blogs are an easy to use and fun way to get English language learners writing, reading, and communicating in English for an *authentic audience.*

For English language learners, it is especially important to document progress over the course of their educational careers. With No Child Left Behind legislation in place throughout the United States, teachers are required to show adequate yearly progress (AYP) for all ELLs. Blogs can help teachers in this respect by offering a space for students to collect their writings over time. The blogs then become virtual portfolios of writing and speaking skills for students. Using a rubric designed especially for evaluating blogs, teachers can demonstrate progress in all four skills. For example:

Quick List

Use blogs for . . .

- Class debates
- Poetry collections
- Creative writing
- Novel or story reviews
- Commenting on essential questions
- Responding to photos of art, historical figures, and audio files of music or speeches
- A detective or suspense short story in installments (different blog posts build on the story over time)
- Group discussions about summer reading
- Writing journals or diaries

- Reading and writing: Students can demonstrate proficiency in writing their own blog and in reading by commenting appropriately on classmates' blogs.
- Speaking and listening: If audio or video files are included in a blog, students can post their own reports, shows, or skits and comment with audio posts on classmates' blogs.

And because blogs are really a vehicle or a tool rather than a specific project or activity, student interactions with blogs can take on many different forms. Educators can use blogs to meet many of the pressing needs related to their own content area, grade level, and educational context.

HOW TO USE BLOGS WITH ELL'S: A SAMPLE BLOG PROJECT

One interesting way for teachers to use blogs with students is through a writing prompt. For example, a teacher might have students view a video, listen to a short lecture or speech, or simply read a provocative statement. The beauty of blogs is that these media can be posted on a teacher's blog prior to class and be ready for a lesson. They can also be made available online for students who are absent from class or who want to review the material at home. On Mr. Horne's middle school ESL class blog (http://esltechnology.com/blog/), the teacher provided students with the stem "If I Ran the . . ." Students chose their own topic and wrote about issues ranging from the dollar store to the world. Here's an example of one student's writing and a subsequent comment by another teacher:

If I Ran the Dollar Store

April 4

Filed under 4th Period, If I Ran the . . . by Salvador
1 comment
If I ran the Dollar Store I'd change a few things. That's just what I'd do.
I will change the toys and put better toys out. I will change the color of the store and change the music they play in the store. I'd sell big cars and hire new people. I would put a theter [sic] and a big park in the Dollar Store and put a skate park offer driving lessons [sic]. I would put a restaurant in the store. I would make a part of the store that has free stuff. I would also put in a sports and a video games store.

Comment: Mrs. Flores April 4

What type of restaurant would you put in the store?

Source: ESLTechnology.com. Accessed August 12, 2009, at http://esltechnology.com/blog/?cat=8

As we can see from the class blog, the actual Web page collects the writing of students across four different periods on the same topic:

Figure 2.3

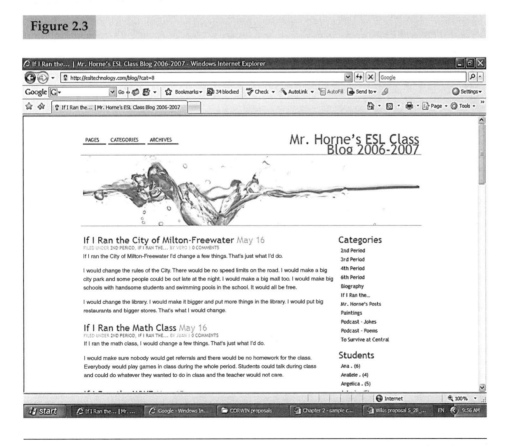

Source: ESLTechnology.com. Accessed on August 12, 2009, at http://esltechnology.com/blog/?cat=8

This project is a good example of how blogs can connect to many different professional goals and standards. By focusing on 21st-century skills, the TESOL standards, and the TESOL technology standards, we can consider blogs and blogging as part of a standards-based curriculum. In the chart that follows, three different tasks that students accomplish in the "If I Ran the . . ." writing project are connected to specific standards.

"If I Ran the . . ." Blog Project: Standards Correlations

Students rethought an established organization (a class, a store, the school) and brainstormed ways to fix existing problems and make innovations and improvements.

21st-Century Skills	TESOL Standards	TESOL Tech Standards
• Creativity and Innovation Skills • Critical Thinking and Problem-Solving Skills • Life and Career Skills: Flexibility and Adaptability • Leadership and Responsibility	• Goal 2, Standard 2: Students use English to obtain, process, construct, and provide subject matter information in spoken and written form. • Goal 2, Standard 3: Students will use appropriate learning strategies to construct and apply academic knowledge.	• Goal 2: Students use technology in socially and culturally appropriate ways.

Students communicated an issue to an audience of readers and received comments and feedback about their writing.

21st-Century Skills	TESOL Standards	TESOL Tech Standards
• Communication and Collaboration Skills • Social and Cross-Cultural Skills	• Goal 3, Standard 1: Students will use the appropriate language variety, register, and genre according to audience, purpose, and setting.	• Goal 3: Students use technology-based tools as aids in the development of their language-learning competence as part of formal instruction and for further learning.

Students utilized word-processing, editing, and uploading skills as a means of sharing ideas.

21st-Century Skills	TESOL Standards	TESOL Tech Standards
• Information, Media and Technology Skills • Initiative and Self-Direction • Productivity and Accountability	• Goal 1, Standard 3: Students will use learning strategies to extend their communicative competence.	• Goal 1: Students demonstrate foundational skills and knowledge in technology for a multilingual world.

Rules for Student Blogging

When starting to blog with students, however, it is important to set up guidelines and rules. Here is an excellent example of blogging rules on Mr. Horne's middle school ESL class blog (http://esltechnology.com/blog/?page_id=59)

Rules for Blogging and Commenting

I don't like too many rules, but if we as a class are going to be using this new technology as a learning tool everyone will be watching us to see how it goes. For this reason, I want very much for this project to run smoothly. The following rules need to be followed at all times when working on our blogs. With *everything* that you write on these pages please remember that *this is for school*, so act like it. Also remember that *I will read everything before it gets published.* There's no way around it, so don't get yourself in trouble. Above all, use this space as a *fun* learning tool.

Rules About Blogging

1. You are expected to treat blogspaces the same as classroom spaces. I expect you to be respectful of everyone.
2. No last names, no telephone numbers, addresses, or even e-mail addresses (in short, don't give out any information that could let a bad guy find you).
3. No pictures without asking first.
4. Don't share your login information and *always* sign out when you're done.
5. Spelling and punctuation matter.
6. You may always write about any *school appropriate* topics. You *may* post outside of class as long as you follow these rules.
7. The more you write the better.

Rules About Commenting on Blogs

1. All the "Rules About Blogging" apply to comments as well.
2. As a student, you must log in to your account to leave comments (that way you don't need to give out an e-mail address).
3. Comments must be well written and have a purpose ("dropping by to say hi" is not a purpose).
4. Please avoid the use of excessive chat lingo whenever possible (lol, ttyl, luv U, me 2, etc.)

Source: ESLTechnology.com. Accessed on August 12, 2009, at http://horne.ws/class/?page_id=3

As we can see from rule number four above, students most likely already blog and send text messages or e-mails. They have already developed proficiency in "chat lingo," or shortened ways of commenting and texting. Here are some examples:

2   =   to, too, or two

U   =   you

W/B   =   write back

LOL   = laughing out loud

WASSUP = what's up?

Since one of the goals of blogging in the school setting is to strengthen the academic writing skills of English language learners, your list of rules might include examples of good writing:

Example of a Good Comment

"Hey, I read what you wrote about Akon. He's my favorite singer too."

Example of a Bad Comment

"HEY U .I JUST WANTED 2 SAY WASUP!!!!!!! CALLME AFTER SKOOL IF U GET DIS P.S W/B TTYL"

Source: ESLTechnology.com. Accessed August 12, 2009, at http://horne.ws/class/?page_id=3

Once students understand the ground rules for blogging, both students and the teacher can begin to explore ways in which blogs can extend and enhance schoolwork for ELLs.

WHEN TO USE BLOGS WITH ELL'S

The previous example of a writing prompt can be used with students across grade levels with some changes made to the amount of writing expected of the student and the prompt to which they are asked to respond. Here are some other examples of grade and age appropriate uses of blogs in the ESL classroom.

Grades K–5

Provide students with a less-open-ended prompt. For example, ask them to ponder what it would be like if they were the teacher and the teacher was a student. Students might also be given a picture prompt rather than a text prompt. A teacher might also decide that instead of having students blog individually, for younger grades they might create a class blog, with the teacher keyboarding the students' responses to a prompt into one blog entry. Beginning students might also be encouraged to record their answer to a prompt orally using a digital recorder.

Grades 6–8

Middle school students are likely to feel motivated by a project in which they are asked to be in charge of something that they would otherwise not control. This type of writing prompt appeals to adolescents who are beginning to find their way in the world. Middle school ELLs might be encouraged to videotape a response to a writing prompt in which they could expand on their ideas about "ruling the school" or running the country. They could be asked to add music to their piece that underscores the feelings expressed in the video. In this way, the middle school student's natural penchant for the dramatic can be put to good use in creating a video blog entry.

Grades 9–12

Older and more experienced students can write a more in-depth response to the "If I Ran the . . ." writing prompt. They can be asked to read their classmates' entries and debate their answers. High school students can be asked to research information relating to their response. For example, if a student decided to respond with "If I Ran the Country . . . ," she might be asked to research the executive branch of the U.S. government and include information and some references in her blog post.

Blogs can be used across all levels with students. As with any Web 2.0 tool, students in the primary grades may require more security measures (more privacy settings, group blogs, etc.) than those on the secondary level. But with an evocative writing prompt—whether text or image—an ESL student on any level can start blogging.

WHO IS USING BLOGS WITH ELL'S?

In this section, you will read about Anne Davis's experience with blogs and her class of ELLs and native English speakers. Anne found that the unique format of blogs allowed for students to feel more connected to a real audience while also providing them the anonymity that some of the more reticent students craved. She reports that her students were more motivated to write and respond to comments when they realized that people from all over the world were actually reading their posts and showing interest in their work.

THINKING AND WRITING WRINKLES BLOGGERS

A group of fifth grade elementary students from J. H. House Elementary School in Conyers, Georgia, who engaged in an educational blogging project titled "Thinking and Writing Wrinkles Bloggers" during the 2003–2004 school year, found that blogging for an authentic audience motivated them to write and write, and write some more. The project's goals were to facilitate the process by which ESL students develop their communicative language skills and to provide students of different ethnic backgrounds the opportunity to learn from each other and from others who read their blogs.

An underlying premise was that blogs could be used as an effective tool to foster cooperative learning between native English-speaking students and ESL students and provide opportunities for increased social, academic, and technological participation. In addition, I felt that the native English-speaking students could also enhance their language skills and have the opportunity to practice helping others with skills they had already internalized. Finally, I was sure that participation in cooperative learning experiences would improve language achievement and interaction between the two groups of students. Blogging did all that and more!

Students were introduced to blogging through the class blog, "Thinking & Writing Wrinkles" (available online at: http://itc.blogs.com/wrinkles). Initially, I posted articles and the students contributed to the class blog through the commenting feature. After a few weeks, each student created his or her own blog. I shared the project with other educational bloggers, who visited the student blogs, read the posts, and, in turn, added their thoughts through the commenting feature. As the students engaged in these discussions, they were really amazed that other people were so interested in what they were writing and learning. The continued dialogue between both students and teachers was incredible. Receiving feedback from others on the comments section of the blog made the students feel valued. When somebody affirmed their thoughts, they were encouraged. The authentic audience motivated the students to believe they had something important to say. They began to show real ownership of the project and they wrote even more.

I used the class blog as a springboard for class discussions. In an excerpt from a post, "Think Possibilities," I encouraged the students' discussions:

I have been reading some very interesting posts from some of my blogging friends this week. They make me think. In turn, I will then write on my blog and others begin to think about what I wrote in response to a friend's post. Sometimes I write about something I have read that makes me want to explore and find out even more about what I think and others think. It's a great way to learn—it's real, it's a way to share and grow with others, and it is an exciting way to learn. Now I have to be motivated, I have to work hard, and I have to really think and write about things of interest to me. What's great about it is that I am part of a community that really cares about education. You won't believe what our main focus is in our edublogging community: it's you guys and all the students from many different states and countries. We view blogs as a place to give you a voice and we want to oversee that process in ways that will make you good thinkers and continue to develop as good citizens of our world. Writing what you think and writing it well can be one of the greatest gifts you can give yourself. You are writing to learn. What's even better is that we can have a lot of fun on the journey.

This type of dialogue, teacher guidance, problem solving, and peer collaboration enhanced the process of using writing to make meaning.

One of the students in the project could speak no English when the year began. Other ESL students translated what we were doing and what we were talking about. He would share his thoughts with us, and a student would help him translate those thoughts into English. He would then blog the translation himself, following our discussions. As the year progressed, he became more and more independent and ended up being one of the "helpers" for other ESL students in the group—a testament to blogging as an effective tool for facilitating language development!

A side blog on idioms was one of the many language experiences built into the project. A place to talk about idioms, their meanings, and their origins—students wrote sentences and stories and illustrated them using idioms in a fun way. This helped the ESL students internalize those hidden meanings. On the blog, students wrote and responded to each other's idioms, providing the needed practice in using the English language. They "got a kick" out of learning idioms and vocabulary usage soared! This love of language led to an end of year ABC book project, "A Book on Blogging" (available online at http://www2.gsu.edu/~coeapd/abc/). Students brainstormed words about blogging, added idioms to the list and created delightful illustrations as you can see from a sample page for the letter "K":

K

K–12, keyboards, knowledge, kids, kind

kick up our heels

K–12 *stands for* **kids** *in kindergarten through 12th grade and we love to blog. People say that young kids can't blog but we disagree. We write good posts with catchy titles and we bump up our writing by using blogs. We type away on the* **keyboards** *on the computers and gain* **knowledge** *as we write. We enjoy getting* **kind** *words from people who have read our blogs. When we get to the lab and find that we have bunches of comments, we celebrate by* **kicking up our heels.**

Figure 2.4

We did "kick up our heels" in joy when the year ended with quite a connection! We even received a post from Pat Street, an author of idioms, who told the students their work was the cat's pajamas!

Source: Used with permission from Anne P. Davis. October 2006. *Learning Technology,* a publication of IEEE Computer Society. Technical Committee on Learning Technology.

MAKE YOUR OWN BLOG

There are countless free sites that offer educators a significant amount of space on which to house your blog. Some of the most popular options are Blogger and WordPress and sites especially for education, like ClassBlogMeister and EduBlogs.

Source: Blogger.com

Source: WordPress.com

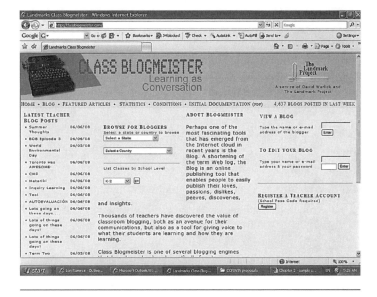

Source: ClassBlogmeister.com

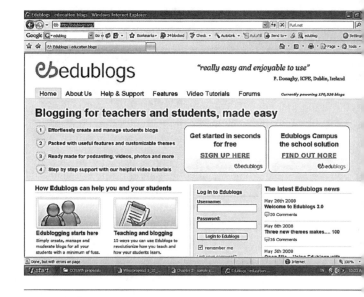

Source: EduBlogs.com

You will find that most of the sites are fairly similar in their services. Here are some questions you might consider when choosing a blog site that works for you:

Is the site intuitive and easy to navigate?

- Is the site visually appealing (i.e., do you like the layout, design, and interface?)
- Does the site have a domain name (URL) that is easy for you to remember?
- Was the site recommended by friends or colleagues who blog?

Once you choose a site to host your blog, sign up for a free account. As with most Web 2.0 tools, you have to choose a unique username and password to be able to create and then continue to log on to your account. It is very important to choose a username and password that you can remember. It might be helpful to write this information down somewhere. There's nothing more frustrating that trying to log on to your blog or wiki (or e-mail, for that matter) and forgetting your username or password! After setting up an account, you can customize your blog—change its color scheme, move columns around, and add features to make it more personalized. On some blogs, you can add pictures, voice, and even video.

Posting to a blog for the first time can seem intimidating. After all, a blog is often public—for all the world to read and then *comment on!* But don't worry too much about mistakes. Most blog sites allow you to redact your posts, or even delete them in order to start over. It is a fairly forgiving medium; so jump in—and *welcome to the blogosphere!*

● ● ●

WHERE TO FIND MORE INFORMATION ABOUT BLOGS

REFERENCES

Davis, A. P. (2006, October). Thinking & writing wrinkles bloggers. *Learning technology.* IEEE Computer Society, Technical Committee on Learning Technology. Retrieved August 13, 2009, from http://www.ieeetclt.org/issues/october 2006/index.html

Deci, E. L., & Ryan, R. M. (1985). *Intrinsic motivation and self-determination in human behavior.* NY: Plenum.

Horne. (2006). *Rules about blogging.* Mr. Horne's ESL class blog 2006–2007. Retrieved August 12, 2009, from http://horne.ws/class/?page_id=3

SUGGESTED READINGS

Camilleri, M., Ford, P., Leja, H., & Sollars, V. (2008). *Blogs: Web journals in language education.* Council of Europe.

Risinger, C. F. (2006, April). Using blogs in the classroom: A new approach to teaching social studies with the internet. *Social Education 70*(3), 130–132. Accessed January 10, 2009, from http://members.ncss.org/se/7003/7003130.pdf

Warlick, D. (2007). *Classroom blogging.* Morrisville, NC: Lulu.com.

HELPFUL WEB SITES

Blogging for ELT—overview and tips for blogging with ELLs: http://www.teachingenglish.org.uk/think/articles/blogging-elt

Conversations About Using Blogs for Teaching ESL—a platform for ESL educators to carry on an ongoing connversation about the ways blogs can be used in the ESL classroom: http://blogs4teachingesl.blogspot.com

How to Create a Blog with Blogger—a video tutorial: http://www.youtube.com/watch?v=BnploFsS_tY

Nik's Learning Technology Blog—tips, resources and teaching materials to help EFL and ESL teachers use ICT and new technology: http://nikpeachey.blogspot.com

Wordpress.com—a step-by-step tutorial on how to blog: http://www.youtube.com/watch?v=MWYi4_COZMU

3

Wikis

Collaboration in a Virtual Space

Video connection: Prior to reading this chapter, view the online video "Wikis in Plain English" at http://www.commoncraft.com/video-wikis-plain-english

WHAT IS A WIKI?

A wiki is a Web page on which many people can add, delete, and edit information. The word *wiki* means "quick" in Hawaiian, and the technology lives up to that name. It is perhaps the quickest way (along with a blog) to upload content to the World Wide Web. For this reason, many people opt to use a wikipage as a simple and fast Web site. Since you don't need to know any programming language (such as HTML or Java), it is the perfect place for a beginner to create a personal or class Web page.

But a wiki can be much more than a Web page. Members of the wiki—either people you have invited or anyone who views it, depending on your privacy settings—can actually take part in building the content of the pages. Members of your wiki community, when signed in properly, can post text, images, audio, and video files to the wiki. They can also *change* information that has already been uploaded—and even delete files. This is the main difference between a wiki and a blog. Posting information to a blog tends to be more proprietary (i.e., someone posts an entry, then readers respond via comments, one after the other); only the "owner" of a blog can create posts, and followers can only make comments. In a wiki environment, however, all members can post information, create pages, change the layout and design of the wiki, and even remove what other members have posted. All members have the ability to post *and* comment.

Perhaps the most famous wiki, Wikipedia, is a good example of what wiki technology can allow users to do. Wikipedia—an online encyclopedia—is a collection of over two and a half million articles on topics ranging from the sublime to the ridiculous. You can find entries on academic topics such as nuclear physics, *The Adventures of Huckleberry Finn,* and polygons. But you may also find entries about people you know, people in the news, and even perhaps an entry about the school in which you teach or learn. (Try it! Go to Wikipedia.org and enter the name of your school in the search box.) The entries have been written and rewritten by experts and nonexperts alike. They might be written by your dentist, your next-door neighbor, or your students—or some combination of all three! Anyone with a computer and access to the Internet can edit entries in this virtual encyclopedia. This may seem counter-intuitive, since technically, your dentist can edit an article about knitting, and your students can add to an article about Szechuan cooking. But is it really such a strange idea?

What makes Wikipedia—and wikis in general—work is its ability to allow for open and transparent collaboration. On Wikipedia, for example, what keeps the dentist from adding erroneous information to the entry on knitting? The answer is simple: the thousands of people who also know a lot about knitting will see errors and take it upon themselves to fix them. Since there are so many people around the world who contribute to Wikipedia, there are also a lot of vigilant editors who don't like to see erroneous information included in their entries. They remove and rewrite information faster than any publishing house could ever revise, print, bind, publish, and distribute a hard copy book version of an encyclopedia. For this reason, Wikipedia—while not meant to be the only source of information on a topic—is often the most up-to-date source, and many believe it to be a good start to any research endeavor.

In schools, Wikipedia has gotten a bad rap. Teachers are wary of the information on the site, since much of it is written by laypeople rather than experts. However, as noted previously, it can be an excellent place to begin a research assignment. With millions of vigilant editors working 24 hours a day to keep information current and correct, users are likely to find the information they need quickly. Using Wikipedia in schools is also a great way to open the topic of media literacy with students. It can spark discussions around heady questions: What information is valid? Who controls the spread of information? How is information disseminated? For further information about using Wikipedia for research, see the suggested readings at the end of this chapter.

But Wikipedia is just one example of what wiki technology can do. Wikis are a great place to plan events, coauthor an article, or do anything that requires the input of more than one person. Since a wiki is a Web site that allows multiple users access to view and edit the same material, it is best used for projects that require collaboration. For example, let's think about starting a book club. The first step might be for all members to choose the books to read in the club. It wouldn't be a very efficient use of time to call a meeting just to decide on a book, so a wiki could be set up with the question, "What books should we read?" All the book club members would be invited to join the wiki and to add to the list. The organizer might post the question along with a suggestion of some books:

Figure 3.1

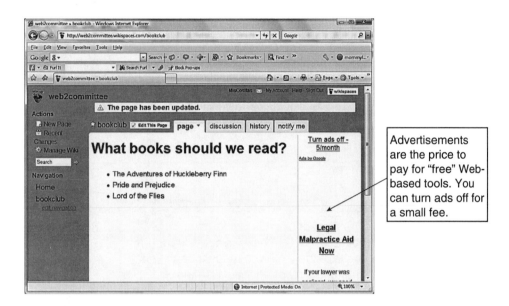

The next member of our theoretical book club may have already read *Pride and Prejudice,* and so she deletes it from the list and adds her own suggestions:

Figure 3.2

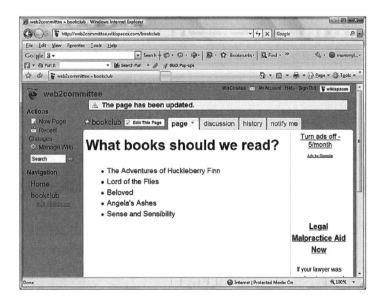

This process continues until everyone has had the chance to weigh in on the subject. What results is a viable list of books that has been "discussed" by everyone in the group. And yet, each member of the group contributed to the list from different locations, at different times of day, and on different days. The "discussion" was asynchronous and yet inclusive of everyone in the group.

Components of a Wiki

More than just a space for collaboration, most wikis have several features that make coauthorship safe and educational. There are toolbars that allow you to create new pages, return to previous versions of the wiki, invite members to join, and, most importantly, edit. Look at the image below for some of the typical components of a wiki.

Figure 3.3

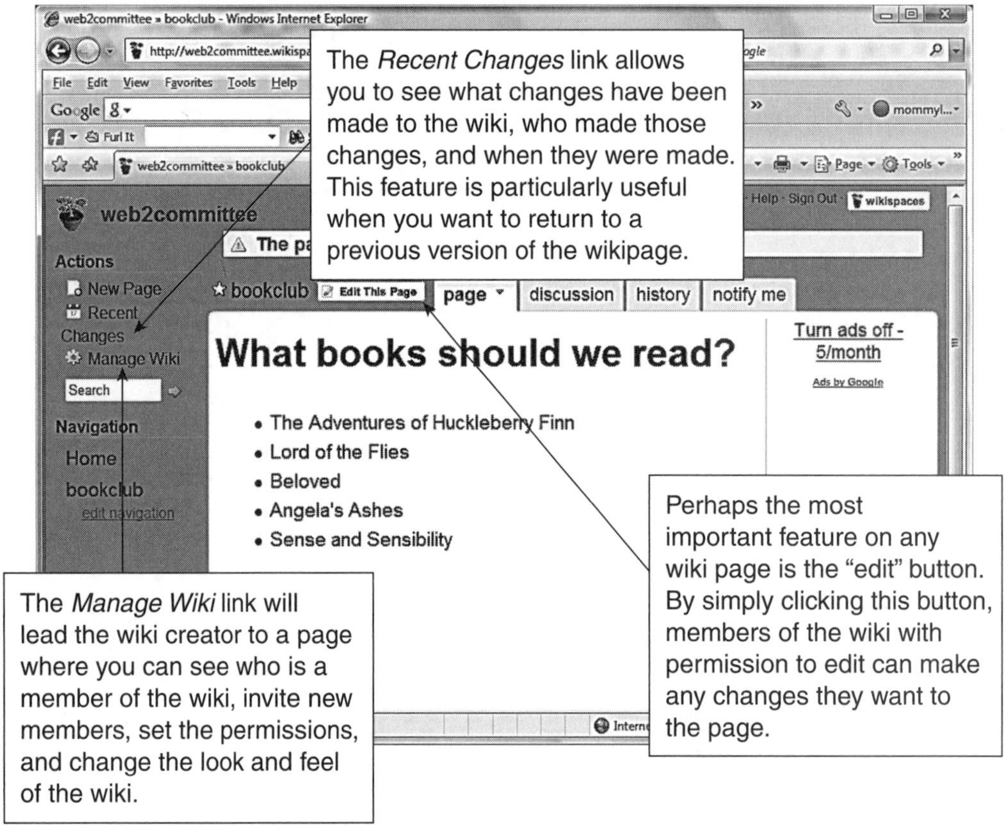
The *Recent Changes* link allows you to see what changes have been made to the wiki, who made those changes, and when they were made. This feature is particularly useful when you want to return to a previous version of the wikipage.
What books should we read?
The Adventures of Huckleberry Finn
Lord of the Flies
Beloved
Angela's Ashes
Sense and Sensibility
Perhaps the most important feature on any wiki page is the "edit" button. By simply clicking this button, members of the wiki with permission to edit can make any changes they want to the page.
The *Manage Wiki* link will lead the wiki creator to a page where you can see who is a member of the wiki, invite new members, set the permissions, and change the look and feel of the wiki.

Source: www.web2committee.wikispaces.com

- **Navigation:** Each time a new page is created, the administrator of a wiki can choose to add a link to that page on the navigation menu. This helps users to find their way to other pages of interest on the wiki.
- **Discussion:** Members of the wiki can communicate via a sort of internal e-mail service or bulletin board. Users type a message in a

way similar to composing an e-mail, and the message gets posted to other users, who can then respond in the same way.

- **History:** This page allows users to see what changes have been made to the wiki. This feature is extremely useful if a wikipage suffers any form of vandalism (i.e., someone posting something inappropriate) or—worse yet—if someone deletes the content of the page (by accident or intentionally). Former incarnations of a wiki are logged and listed chronologically on this page so that the administrator can simply repost the version of the page immediately prior to the accident or vandalism—sort of like a wiki time machine!

- **Notifications:** Users can sign up for instant notifications via e-mail whenever a page on a wiki has been edited. This is useful for teachers and helps to keep track of the changes being made to a site.

Posting on Wikis

As with blogs, wiki posts can be open or private. Most wiki sites allow members to choose among the following settings (these terms are specifically from Wikispaces, but other sites use similar terminology):

Wiki Permissions	
Level	**Description**
Public	Everyone can view pages; anyone—including nonmembers—can edit pages. ☑ Allow message posts from non-members.
Protected	Everyone can view pages; only members of this wiki can edit pages. ☑ Allow message posts from non-members.
Private	Only members of this wiki can view and edit pages.

Source: www.wikispaces.com

Notice that each level of protection refers to three elements of the wiki: who can view pages, who can edit pages, and who can post messages. There is often a charge for private sites (Wikispaces offers a private site for free for the first 30 days, but there is a charge after that time).

As was the case with blogs, the more open a wiki, the more the likelihood of students receiving information, comments, and even edits from a variety of worldwide audiences. For example, consider a wiki created by students about endangered species. An unexpected edit or comment to the wiki from a biologist working with polar bears in Alaska would be a welcomed addition to the project. That might not happen were the blog to be too protected from outside viewing and commenting. As is with all Web 2.0 tools, however, it is important for the teacher to choose the level of privacy that is comfortable for each individual school or classroom context.

WHY READ OR WRITE A WIKI WITH ELL'S?

In the classroom, a wiki becomes a space for students to collaborate on group projects. Wikis allow ELLs to coconstruct meaning on a variety of writing projects such as essays, reports, and group projects from different locations almost simultaneously. As with blogs, wikis allow for students to collaborate without actually meeting face to face—a benefit for those shy newcomers and students who cannot meet after school or on weekends.

Oftentimes as teachers, we hear concerns from students about having enough time to meet with their lab partners or project buddies. The barriers to meeting together run the gamut from no transportation to no time. Working on a group assignment becomes much more feasible when everyone can work from home by collaborating via a wiki. For example, one student can upload her data notes from a biology lab to the wiki. Her lab partner can then upload photos from the lab. They can both write observations, analysis of the data, and conclusions on the same wiki page—both from the convenience of their own homes. One lab partner can edit the other's spelling. The second lab partner might suggest a rephrasing of a sentence or two. In this way, these two students can coauthor their lab report. Students can do peer editing of creative writing, critique each other's history essays, share photos of their artwork in a virtual gallery, and even coauthor poetry on a wiki.

Being able to collaborate from different physical places on a joint project or report is an exciting idea for students. In the 21st-century workplace, more and more people are telecommuting and performing many job-related duties from the comfort of their own homes. Students can now take advantage of technology to collaborate with their classmates from home—and with students from other parts of the world as well. When students collaborate and create art, poetry, research, and other projects with students from other countries, they are learning communication and collaboration skills—one of the 21st-century skills that they will need in an ever growing global marketplace. They are learning to become flexible by accepting edits and rewrites from classmates while strengthening social and crosscultural skills by learning how to best communicate with people whose backgrounds may be very different from their own. As multiple voices express a variety of ideas and viewpoints via a wiki, students must learn to collaborate as they all work towards a common goal. Leadership skills are strengthened when students are faced with the challenge of taking the lead on a topic, editing material that is either poorly written or erroneous, and even deciding whether or not to acccept a coauthor's edits on a particular project.

There are thousands of wikis already available for viewing, commenting, and even editing online. Students might begin with an analysis of the most famous wiki, Wikipedia. They might even try their hand at editing an entry on a topic about which they are familiar. They might then move to a wiki created by another class or school and comment on its contents. By exploring preexisting wikis, students will have the opportunity to understand the various features before setting out to create one of their own.

Wikis, like blogs, if created as a public space, can be open to edits and comments from many different users. For example, teachers in other disciplines can log on and make edits, suggest alternate vocabulary or grammatical structures, or just simply give feedback on students' work. In all subject areas, that elusive one-on-one teacher meeting time is so important in developing writing skills and understanding of often challenging content for ELLs. With a wikipage dedicated, for example, to a social studies essay, ESL students can write a draft that can be peer edited by classmates as well as by their social studies teacher. The use of wikis in this way extends the time that ELLs can "meet" with their teachers. It also gives them text feedback that some will be able to process better than the oral feedback provided in a classroom face-to-face meeting.

Most wiki sites will allow students to collect their work over time and give them the possibility of organizing it in ways that make sense to the individual user. ELLs can open a separate wikipage for each subject area and have these spaces available for collaborative work with peer tutors, classmates, and their teachers. This work can remain on the site over time and then be used as the basis for a virtual portfolio— complete with detailed accounts of all edits, additions, deletions, and comments. An ELL's wikispace can become a repository for her work over the period of a year—and might serve as the basis for an exit or graduation portfolio as well.

Quick List

Use wikis for . . .

- Webquests
- Collaborative projects
- Coauthoring of essays or reports
- Interactive games (e.g., "what would you do next . . ." games)
- Planning for a class event (e.g., a party, a festival, or a celebration)
- Sign-up sheets for events
- Quick and easy Web sites with links and resources
- Online study communities
- A place to post and share student work (e.g., scanned art images and writing)

HOW TO USE WIKIS WITH ELL'S: A SAMPLE WIKI PROJECT

A wiki is an appropriate tool for any project that requires collaboration among students. For example, consider a project in which students are asked to create a story together. The teacher could give students the beginning part of the story (or even the first few chapters) and then ask students to add parts to it. The nice part of creating a story in this way is that, through links to other pages, students can create "back stories" by creating information about peripheral characters in the story, telling their stories too. You could start this off by creating or copying a short story or fairy tale and creating new pages for each of the other characters. Students could then be encouraged to tell the story from the perspective of these characters. For example, students could tell the story of Cinderella from the point of view of an ugly sister, or from the rat that got turned into a horse. This is a good way to develop some creative thinking skills and help students see things from different perspectives.

Here is an example of this activity using *Cinderella* as the story:

Figure 3.4

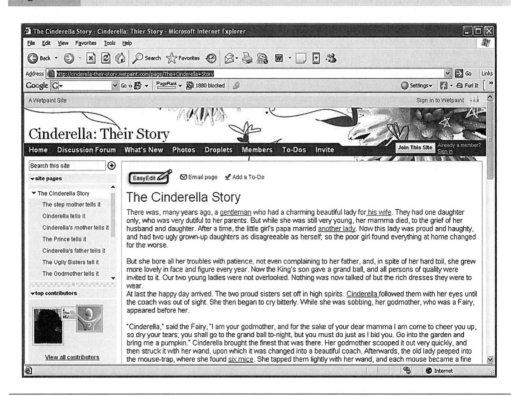

Source: Used with permission from Nik Peachey. http://nikpeachey.blogspot.com/2008/05/using-wikis-with-efl-students.html). Accessed January 27, 2009, at http://cinderella-their-story.wetpaint.com/

Some possible tasks that students could do using this wiki include

- Adding some adjectives and adverbs to the text;
- Adding an extra sentence to one of the background stories;
- Inventing a new character for the story;
- Finding words that you don't understand and adding them to the glossary;
- Adding some definitions to some of the glossary words;
- Writing questions that you would like to ask one of the characters and putting them into the "to do" list; and
- Looking for questions that someone else has asked about the text and trying to include that information in your version of the story.

This project is a good example of how wikis can allow students to explore multiple perspectives and include their own voices along with those of others. Students are able to read the work of classmates and then elaborate or change the details to create some new information. This type of project fits in well with the 21st Century Skills, the TESOL Standards, and the TESOL Technology Standards, as can be seen from the chart below.

"The Cinderella Story" Wiki Project: Standards Correlations

Students read a familiar fairy tale and were asked to pay attention to the different perspectives of the various characters.		
21st-Century Skills	**TESOL Standards**	**TESOL Tech Standards**
• Creativity and Innovation Skills • Critical Thinking and Problem-Solving Skills • Communication and Collaboration Skills • Life and Career Skills: Flexibility and Adaptability • ICT Literacy	• Goal 2, Standard 2: Students use English to obtain, process, construct, and provide subject matter information in spoken and written form. • Goal 3, Standard 1: To use English in socially and culturally appropriate ways: Students will use the appropriate language variety, register, and genre according to audience, purpose, and setting.	• Goal 1: Students demonstrate foundational skills and knowledge in technology for a multilingual world. • Goal 2: Students use technology in socially and culturally appropriate ways.

Students find words that are unfamiliar to them, investigate their meaning, and add definitions to the glossary.		
21st-Century Skills	**TESOL Standards**	**TESOL Tech Standards**
• Critical Thinking and Problem Solving Skills • Information Literacy • Initiative and Self-Direction • Productivity and Accountability	• Goal 2, Standard 2: Students use English to obtain, process, construct, and provide subject matter information in spoken and written forms. • Goal 2, Standard 3: Students will use appropriate learning strategies to construct and apply academic knowledge.	• Goal 3: Students use technology-based tools as aids in the development of their language-learning competence as part of formal instruction and for further learning.

Students were asked to pay attention to questions asked in other versions of the story and to try to incorporate them into their own.		
21st-Century Skills	**TESOL Standards**	**TESOL Tech Standards**
• Critical Thinking and Problem-Solving Skills • Communication and Collaboration Skills • Flexibility and Adaptability	• Goal 3, Standard 1: To use English in socially and culturally appropriate ways: Students will use the appropriate language variety, register, and genre according to audience, purpose, and setting. • Goal 1, Standard 3: Students will use learning strategies to extend their communicative competence.	• Goal 1: Students demonstrate foundational skills and knowledge in technology for a multilingual world. • Goal 2: Students use technology in socially and culturally appropriate ways.

Rules for Student Wiki Pages

Since wikis offer students a great deal of freedom and power to change, edit, and delete content, it is crucial to set up rules for appropriate use in the ESL classroom. Here is an excellent list of rules for wiki etiquette from one of the wiki providers, PB Wiki:

Wiki Etiquette for Students: How to Act on a Wiki

Keep safe. Never post your personal information or information about someone else. Keep things like ages, addresses, phone numbers, names of towns, or even places we work off the Internet. Remember that information on the Internet, especially embarrassing information, may still be around after you've deleted it. Be careful not to post things that may come back to haunt you later.

Be truthful. Write things you know to be correct using facts from research *from reliable, credible sources.*

Ask first, then give credit. Ask an artist's permission to post their photos, pictures, or pieces of writing. Never use first and last names of people that could identify them in a photo or video. You must also ask permission when using an idea from a friend, a family member, or even from an acquaintance. After you have his/her permission, then you must ask if you can post his/her name to give him/her credit. If you know anyone who is breaking any part of this rule, it is very important to tell someone who can help immediately.

Be nice. The most important thing to remember is sarcasm hurts. Be overly friendly and be positive. Remember . . . treat others as you would like to be treated.

Read, reread, and proofread before you click ENTER. Don't rush to make that final. Once you press that button, you can't bring it back. Look everything over and use your spell check to be sure everything is accurate. When you are certain that the editing is complete, then *save* to publish.

Information please. The Internet is a great source of information but information is only useful when it is accurate.

Be brief, to the point, and logical. Use breaks in your text and formatting elements to make the page easy to read and understand.

Follow directions. Be sure to follow the directions that are given for the assignment—be creative, but within the parameters set forth on the page.

Do not delete the work of others deliberately unless it is part of the editing process.

Keep it on topic—classroom oriented. This isn't the place to discuss afterschool plans.

Source: Accessed on January 6, 2009, at http://educators.pbwiki.com/Wiki+Etiquette+for+Students

It is also helpful to have students think about and comment on some of the rules for participating in a wiki, as did Ms. G, a sixth-grade teacher in Waikiki, Hawaii. Here, one of her students comments on their class wiki *about* posting on their class wiki! Notice that two students and the teacher herself posted follow-up comments like: "luv what u wrote," and "MH, you used examples in your explanations, good job. It's great that you created all the links for each assignment." Also notice that, for security purposes, this teacher and her school have opted to use initials of the students and the teacher rather than using their actual names.

Rules of Wiki and of Etiquette for Students

Page history last edited by mhc8 4 months ago

The things I learned are that your not supposed to put personal information about your self. I also learned that I'm supposed to be truthful on the wiki and I'm not supposed to tell a lie and what ever it is it might come back to me like say I am telling a lie to Taylor and then she starts to tell a lie back to me. Another thing I learned is that i have to watch out like if I use my real name and then someone like tracks me down man that is SCARY! That is what i learned about the wiki rules.

Here is the actual wikipage:

Figure 3.5

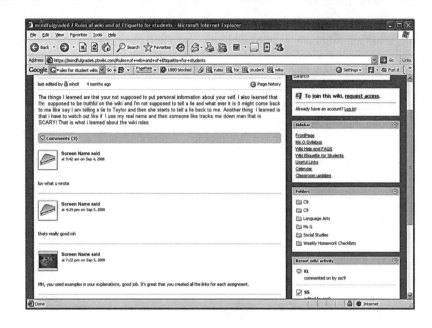

Source: Used with permission from Valerie Gee. MindfulGrade6.pbworks.com. Boxed text and screenshot accessed on 1/6/09 at https://mindfulgrade6.pbwiki.com/Rules+of+wiki+and+of+Etiquette+for+students

By designing activities like this one in which students comment about the use of these new media and how their participation might be viewed by others, teachers can help strengthen not just language skills but also media literacy and technology skills in English language learners.

WHEN TO USE WIKIS WITH ELL'S

Rewriting a story or a piece of text using a wiki is an excellent means of using wiki technology at any grade level. Here are some other activities that can be used at a variety of grade and proficiency levels.

Grades K–5

Class wikis can be set up for different stories, having separate pages within each tale for vocabulary, useful expressions, and grammatical structures. Students can add illustrations corresponding to the stories, photos of themselves reading or acting out the stories, and, for literate students, reviews of the tales and opinion pieces about the morals of the stories (e.g., Do you agree with the ending of the story? Why or why not?)

Grades 6–8

Teachers can use a wiki to create an online course book by collaborating with other teachers or with students. Students could select texts and subjects that they are interested in and type or paste them in to pages on the wiki. In this way, adolescent students, who often exhibit poor study or organizational skills, are encouraged to create their very own learning materials to go with the text. Students can also add extra information and background on a theme or topic and add grammar and vocabulary that goes with the text. Another good activity for middle school students is a collaboration with a school in another town—or better still, another country. Teachers could use the wiki as a cultural research tool with students researching the country and the culture of their partner students to create a wiki about it. The partner students could then correct or comment on any errors or misunderstandings of their culture.

Grades 9–12

Since wikis have many of the same communication features (such as e-mail lists and discussions), an online discussion (or forum) could be established for students to discuss the story and make decisions about how they want to change or develop it. Students could upload or link to videos or images. Teachers could use the "To do" feature of the wiki to set up tasks for different groups or students.

Wikis are a wonderful tool for students to work together and produce high-quality texts. They are also great if you want to be able to share students' work with parents and the rest of the world, or just limit access to your class.

WHO IS USING WIKIS WITH ELL'S?

In this section, we will learn about Kathleen Mitchell's experience using wikis with her English language learners. Despite some initial trepidation, Kathleen shares her process of learning how to use wikis in her classroom and the subsequent unbridled excitement of her students.

WIKIFIED

When I first set up my class wiki, I had no idea what was going to happen. I was a little bit of a technophobe, but I wanted to make our computer lab time worthwhile. The only thing I knew was that I wanted the wiki to be the students' place. It wasn't supposed to be "the teacher's Web site." It was theirs. So I decided we would learn how to use the wiki together, one skill per week. The first day was spent just typing stories on the wiki. Still, it was exciting. Most of my students didn't know who wrote text for the Internet. They were thrilled to learn that they could write on the Web. And that's how it started—slowly with students typing stories. But the wiki soon took on a life of its own.

During an activity where students wrote quizzes for each other, I looked over my student's shoulder and noticed that the quiz he was writing for his classmates was picture based. Each question had a picture and asked students to describe it. I thought it was brilliant. I hadn't taught students how to add pictures to the wiki. It wasn't even on the schedule to teach, but suddenly everyone wanted to know how to do it! By the end of that class, this ESL student had taught everyone how to add pictures to their pages. And as a class, we had an impromptu debate about which picture should be on our wiki's homepage. That day, there was a clear language learning benefit to using the wiki. It led students to practice explaining and persuading. But more than that it engaged students and let them be the experts. All of this happened without my planning. It happened because the students were creative and quick to learn the technology. It also happened because I let it happen—it was a true "teachable moment."

My message to my ESL colleagues is this: Don't think you have to know a lot in order to use a new technology. The same goes for planning lessons to use with the wiki. A lot of normal classroom activities can be "wikified." I have had students write quizzes on the wiki and then have other students take the quizzes. Students have also edited each other's work and created personal dictionaries. The activities don't have to be something new; just think about how you can take advantage of all the features wikis have to offer to modify and improve an activity that you already use in your classes.

It's helpful to understand that wikis are time and space independent. Take for example editing papers: Usually students swap papers, which means absences and odd-numbers can create problems. However, on a wiki, odd numbers aren't a problem, and no one can lose their essay because it's online. Secondly, it is very easy to track students' progress because you can see every draft of a document and easily compare drafts. This is helpful for grading, peer-editing and group work, but also for individual work.

This brings me to the third and most famous benefit of wikis: They are a great way to collaborate. It can be difficult to sustain group work over multiple class periods. Students often forget what they were doing or where their notes were, and it's hard to write a document together. On a wiki, on the other hand, all of the group information is in one place. They can all edit the page, and as a teacher, I can know exactly who contributed what to the final product. So not only do wikis make group work easier, but they make assessing group work easier.

One more benefit of wikis is the fact that wikis are less immediate and dependent on the classroom. Presenting in front of the classroom makes some students very anxious. It can be embarrassing for a student to read a paper to the class or share their work in a face-to-face context. On a wiki though, there is less immediacy and it can be less personal. Students don't see their peer's reactions to their work in the form of facial expressions and gestures. They don't have to hand them their paper. At any given moment, they might not even know that someone is reading their work, and that unexpected reader might leave them an encouraging comment. So without being put on the spot to share, they can get encouragement and feedback in a less intimidating way.

Let me give you an example of a lesson that really took advantage of the benefits of the wiki—an adaptation of a typical writing activity. In my class, students often write an essay and then share it with a classmate. With their partner, students work on content and conventions and then write a final draft. We went through a similar process on the wiki, but I decided to also use audio clips throughout the lesson so that students with low literacy skills could still assess the content of the essay and students with low speaking skills still got to share orally. Students began by recording themselves reading their essays. They were allowed to record it as many times as they wanted so that they felt confident and comfortable. Some students, after listening to their recordings, noticed some errors and asked for specific pronunciation help. In a traditional setting, I doubt that students would have felt comfortable enough interrupting pair work to learn how to more accurately pronounce a word. However, while recording themselves, students focused on speaking accurately and felt comfortable asking questions. When they were finished, I helped them post their audio clip on the essay page of the wiki and asked them to listen to another student's clip. Interestingly enough, because wikis are time and space independent, it didn't matter if the other student, whose essay they were reading, was present in class, or even at the same point in the activity. While listening to the audio clip, students had the ability to pause and replay it as many times as they wanted. This helped students develop their listening skills. It would be uncomfortable to ask a person to repeat him- or herself several times, but students had that opportunity on the wiki and they took advantage of it. After hearing the essay, they posted a comment on their classmate's page. In the comment, they were asked to restate the essay's main idea, give supporting evidence, and list a few favorite features of the essay. Once students received comments on their essay's content, they made revisions, retyped their essay, and posted it to the wiki. In some cases, they made revisions so that the main idea was clearer. Next, a peer went back and read the typed essay. They edited the page for any grammatical or spelling errors. Again they left a comment on what they had changed and what their peer had done well. The author went back one more time to look for errors and improvements and compare drafts. Finally, they printed out their essays and turned them in. While the time each individual spent on the activities varied because of the options to rerecord and relisten, all of the students finished within four hours (two computer lab sessions).

Their reactions to the lesson were positive, but it took time for them to feel comfortable. At the beginning of the lesson, some students didn't like listening to themselves on the recording. Those students usually recorded themselves several times. One of my more anxious students called me over after recording a few time times, and his whole perception of his speaking had changed. He wanted me to listen to how good he sounded! While they were uncomfortable recording themselves, having the option to rerecord eased most students' fears.

Students also loved to listen to other student's essays. Sometimes we listen to clips from Randall's ESL Cyber Listening lab (www.esl-lab.com). In another wiki activity, instead of listening to strangers from the listening lab, students got to listen to their peers. They really enjoyed it. However, leaving comments on the essay about content was difficult for some students. Fixing conventions was easier for them. Students said they liked just typing in the corrections, instead of "writing all over" someone's paper. It felt as if they found editing on the wiki to be less disrespectful than editing on paper. Students also seemed to receive the changes well. They liked that they didn't have to go back and change a lot of things because the changes were already there. At the same time, they could change the view and see exactly what edits their peers had made. I noticed that some students didn't change the view of their page, so that they could see the edits more clearly. That led me to believe that they were reflecting on the suggestions even more so than with traditional paper edits.

What did they learn? Students practiced speaking, listening, writing, reading, and grammar. Specifically with speaking, they practiced using suprasegmental stress and segmental issues in words. This activity was not comprehensive enough for long-term speech modification, but it did raise awareness of problems and taught them to pronounce words that they commonly write, but never say. For example, students don't say "however," but some students wrote it. In this activity, they learned how it was pronounced. Their listening skills were also improved. Most students demonstrated their ability to listen for the main idea and supporting ideas. In writing, students showed clear and systematic organization of their essays. They also worked on writing conventions. Some of the writing conventions were actually grammatical issues. They were able to find and correct mistakes in their peers' work, and they demonstrated their ability to write a comprehensible and grammatically cohesive essay.

Through this lesson, each student ended up having a polished final draft. I was impressed by their abilities. The wiki seemed to help them focus. And it enhanced the listening and speaking outcomes of the lesson. In a normal setting, I don't think either of those would have been significant. Overall, this lesson allowed for learner differences, like proficiency and anxiety. It allowed learners to work at their own speed and on troublesome areas, which are different for each learner. The wiki allowed them to help each other without worrying about the social ramifications of correcting someone. Most importantly, the wiki helped them meet these learning objectives in a safe and engaging environment. Now I am exploring more ways in which to "wikify" more activities in my ESL classroom.

Source: Kathleen Mitchell, personal correspondence, 2009.

MAKE YOUR OWN WIKI

Setting up a wiki is a quick process. With the multitude of wiki sites available, there are many options for your personal or school-based wikispace. Some of the most popular wiki hosts for educators are Wikispaces, WetPaint, and PBWiki. Google also has a wiki option called Google Sites.

Source: Wikispaces.com

Source: PBWiki.com

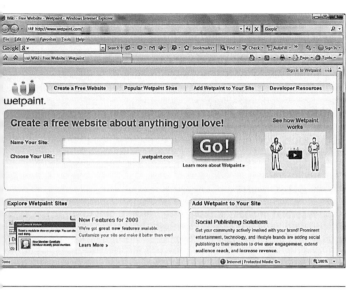

Source: WetPaint.com

Source: GoogleSites.com

Each of these sites offers free wiki hosting with the opportunity to establish your own unique Web site URL (e.g., www.myveryown wiki.wikispaces.com). Most of the wiki hosting sites publish ads on your wiki that you will have no control over; however WetPaint and WikiSpaces offer "ad-free wikis" for educational purposes. On other wikis, for a nominal fee (approximately $5/month), you can "turn off" these ads.

Once you choose a site to host your wiki, you sign up for a free account. Choose a unique username and password and then continue to log on to your account. After you set up an account, you can customize your wiki. Most sites allow you to change colors or themes, add pages, invite members, and organize your information.

To post information to your wiki for the first time, look for the "edit this page" button, and click. This will open a window into which you can type your information. (Don't forget to save drafts often.) After you are satisfied with your post, click "save" and you will exit from the editing screen to view the finished product.

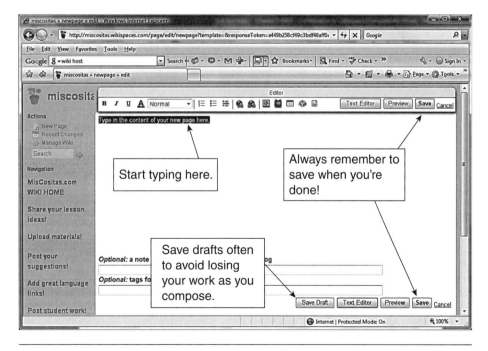

Source: Wikispaces.com

After you upload information, you will want to invite members so that they will also be able to edit your wiki. Click on the "manage wiki" link to invite members via e-mail. Once they are invited—and accepted by you—as members, they will have almost all the same rights as you do to edit your pages. If any editing takes place that you don't agree with or would like to remove, you can always keep track of—and retrieve—previous versions of the wiki by clicking on the "history" tab.

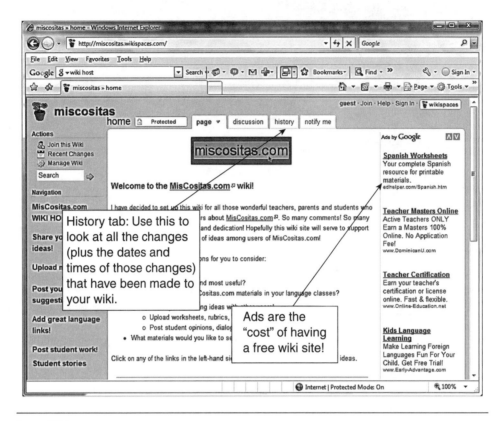

Source: Wikispaces.com

Sharing information on a wiki is a fun and exciting way to collaborate online. How can you "wikify" your ESL classroom?

● ● ●

WHERE TO FIND MORE INFORMATION ABOUT WIKIS

SUGGESTED READINGS

Borja, R. R. (2006, April 4). Educators experiment with student-written 'wikis.' *Education Week, 25*(30), 10.

Jakes, D. (2006, August 15). Wild about wikis. *Technology & Learning.* Retrieved August 13, 2009, from http://www.techlearning.com/article/6164

Sze, P. (2008, January). Online collaborative writing using wikis. *The Internet TESL Journal, 15*(1). Retrieved August 13, 2009, from http://iteslj.org/Techniques/Sze-Wikis.html

West, J. A., & West, M. L., (2008). *Using wikis for online collaboration: The power of the read-write web (online teaching and learning series (OTL)).* Somerset, NJ: Jossey-Bass Publishers.

Researching with Wikipedia. (2009, July 10). Wikipedia: The free encyclopedia. Retrieved August 13, 2009, from http://en.wikipedia.org/wiki/Wikipedia: Researching_with_Wikipedia

HELPFUL WEB SITES

Curriki—this is a wiki with resources for teachers such as lesson plans, curriculum documents, and forums for educators www.curriki.org

Examples of Educational Wikis: http://educationalwikis.wikispaces.com/ Examples+of+educational+wikis

What Can PB Wiki Do For You?—a video tutorial about PBWiki in Education: http://pbwiki.com/content/viewdemo

Wikispaces video tour—including Introduction, Personalize your Wiki, Files and Pictures, Notification and RSS, and Personal Settings: http://www.wikispaces .com/site/tour#introduction

4

Podcasts

Get Them Talking!

Video connection: Prior to reading this chapter, view the online video "Podcasting in Plain English" at http://www.commoncraft.com/podcasting

WHAT IS A PODCAST?

According to Wikipedia, a podcast is "a series of audio or video digital-media files which is distributed over the Internet by syndicated download, through Web feeds, to portable media players and personal computers" (accessed August 15, 2009, at http://en.wikipedia.org/wiki/Podcast).

But more simply put, a podcast is like a radio show on your computer. It can consist of one episode or a series of shows connected by a common theme. Technically, to be a podcast, the audio files must contain an RSS (really simple syndication) feed that will allow users to download new episodes when they are added to a Web site. In this way, new shows get transferred onto mp3 audio players (your iPod) automatically when you connect one to your computer.

But not all podcasts need to be downloaded onto an mp3 player. Furthermore, you don't need an iPod (Apple's version of a digital audio file player) to listen to a podcast. Most podcasts will play directly on your computer, and you can listen to some episodes and not others without subscribing to an automatic feed. Here's an easy way to think about podcasts: Imagine a magazine that you like to read. You can subscribe to the magazine and get a copy mailed to your home every month. You can also go to the library and choose a particular issue to read any time you want.

At the library, there are back issues as well. It is a similar process with podcasts. Subscribe if you want. If not, just listen to the parts you like online. Podcasts, like blogs and wikis, come in all shapes and sizes. There are podcasts to help you learn Chinese (www.chinesepod.com) and podcasts about vegetarian cooking (www.compassionatecooks.com). Podcasts are created by professionals (like National Public Radio's "This American Life" www.thisamericanlife.org) and by amateurs (www.homemadehit show.com). There is likely to be a podcast that relates to almost any topic that is taught in school.

Components of a Podcast

Once you find a podcast that you'd like to hear, you have some choices. First, ask yourself if you'd like to subscribe to the podcast, or would you just like to listen to it? Listening to a podcast on the computer is as simple as clicking "Play" (or the universal symbol for "play," the sideways triangle: ▶). In order to subscribe to a podcast, look for the orange RSS symbol: (or the letters RSS: RSS 2.0).

Figure 4.1

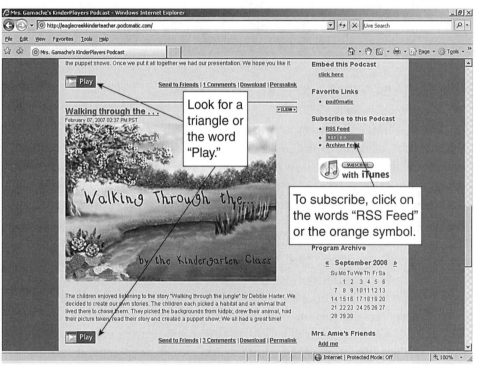

Source: Used with permission from Amie Gamache. Accessed on 12/26/08 at EagleCreekKinderTeacher .podomatic.com/

Since podcasts are often embedded into blogs, many of the same features that appear on blogs can be seen alongside podcasts as well. For example:

- **Comment:** Listeners can comment about the podcast, and these comments are often displayed directly after the original post. They often display the time and date the comment was posted and the screen name, user ID, or possibly the e-mail address of whoever leaves comments.
- **Profile:** The creator of the podcasts will usually have some area dedicated to personal and/or school information. A description of the podcast project is also often included in the profile.
- **Archive/Links:** In a sidebar or side column, there can be links to other podcasts. These links can be arranged by the name or topic of the podcast or by date the podcast was created.

Creating a Podcast

Consuming (listening to) podcasts is just half the story. Making podcasts is where the fun lies for students. A podcast can be created on any topic—it is limited only to your imagination! Students should start by storyboarding their podcast, much in the way they outline a story or research project before writing. Students create a script or a series of questions they plan to ask an interviewee. They might also consider any background music, visuals, or sound effects that they would want to include in a podcast.

After planning the content of a podcast, all that is needed is some simple technology to create one:

- A computer with Internet connection
- Speakers (either external or your computer's internal speaker)
- A microphone (either external or built in)
- A digital recorder (optional)
- An iPod or other mp3 player with a microphone (optional)

Students can record interviews, stories, autobiographies, or journal entries into a digital recorder or directly onto the computer using a microphone (note: on some computers, there is a built-in microphone that can be used). Using free programs like Audacity (www.audacity.com), students can edit the audio file and upload it to a Web page, a blog entry, or a wiki. They can also use podcast-hosting sites like PodOMatic (www.podomatic .com) to upload, organize, and share their podcasts. Here are some options that PodOMatic offers to users:

Figure 4.2

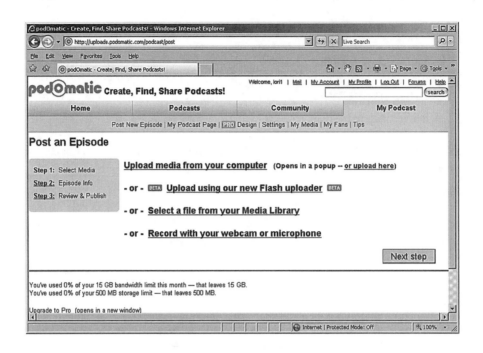

Source: PodOMatic.com. Accessed December 26, 2008, at http://uploads.podomatic.com/podcast/post

PodOMatic will walk you through the steps of posting your podcast to the World Wide Web. It will offer options such as writing a description of the podcast, adding photos, and including tags (keywords that will help others to find your podcast on the Web). See the "Make Your Own Podcast" section later in this chapter for more details on setting up a podcast for yourself or your classes.

Once your podcast is up and running, anyone with an Internet connection can listen in!

WHY LISTEN TO AND CREATE PODCASTS WITH ELL'S?

Podcasts abound on the Internet. There are podcasts on almost every subject you can dream of—and they are excellent, authentic listening resources for English language learners. Whether a podcast was created expressly for ELLs or just designed for listeners with common interests, podcasts can provide students with information, aural practice, and accent training. Listening to podcasts from different regions of the world, different parts of the country, and even different neighborhoods in your city or town can provide students with exposure to different accents, a variety of registers, and access to colloquial and formal expressions. Furthermore, they are just plain engaging to listen to (the good ones, at least!).

As with blogs and wikis, however, it's fun to read and listen to podcasts, but it's much more fun—and more pedagogically rich—for students to create their own podcasts and publish them to the Web. When students know that their voices can be heard by their parents at home or by their relatives back in their home country, they feel motivated to create dynamic and polished podcasts. Access to an international audience is again one of the best ways to inspire students to create great work.

Beginning ELLs who may be going through their silent period may feel more comfortable speaking into a microphone in a corner of the classroom or at home rather than speaking in front of a class of peers. They can record—and rerecord—their podcasts until they are satisfied with the results, thus exerting more control over the final product and building their confidence levels with regard to their speaking and listening skills.

Students can edit and rearrange their sound files. They can be creative and allow their artistic sides to flourish by adding images and music to support the content of their podcast. They can embed their podcasts into blogs or wikis or post them onto their own homepage or Web site. In other words, podcasting allows students to tap in to a variety of intelligences (Gardner, 1983):

- *Linguistic:* Students write scripts, create dialogs and stories, and develop characters.
- *Logical-mathematical:* Students create a storyboard with a sequence of scenes and edit audio files. They time sequences and add images to correspond with different segments of the audio script.
- *Musical:* Students add music to set a tone or underscore a particular theme or mood of the podcast.
- *Interpersonal:* Students interview classmates, family, and community members.
- *Intrapersonal:* Students create an autobiographical podcast in which they reflect on a particular aspect of their lives. Students can develop a "podcast diary" and share daily reflections on a variety of topics.
- *Visual-spatial:* Students can choose digital photos to support meaning at different points in their podcast in order to create an enhanced podcast.

Podcasts engage students' talents and skills in so many ways. Once a class learns the mechanics of creating and posting a podcast, podcasting can be incorporated into every discipline in the school.

Quick List

Use podcasts for . . .

- Weather reports
- Science reports
- Poetry recitation
- Pronunciation practice
- Classroom news
- Old-time radio soap operas
- Interviews with parents, teachers, community members
- Directions to a place in school or in the community

HOW TO USE PODCASTS WITH ELL'S: A SAMPLE PODCAST PROJECT

Having students document the lives of community members is a wonderful way of strengthening questioning and investigative skills in students while also validating the community at large by bringing members of the community into the school environment. In this project, we see how a pair of teachers chose to highlight and document the exceptional lives of women in one Wisconsin town.

When wonderful student podcasts "go viral" (become extremely popular and spread via the World Wide Web), it is exciting to see them take on a life of their own. This is what happened with the "Coulee Kids" podcasts (http://wiki.lacrosseschools.org/groups/couleekids/)—a collection of reports and newscasts created by seventh graders at the Longfellow Middle School in LaCrosse, Wisconsin. The student podcasts have been highlighted in articles in mainstream and educational media from the *New York Times* (Selingo, 2006) to *Education Week* (Borja, 2005). Students create podcasts on topics ranging from poetry to geography.

A recent Coulee Kids project involves students in researching and interviewing the everyday heroes who live in their own community. Their homepage describes the project:

When meandering down the road of life, we encounter special people that positively impact our lives. We have the opportunity to thank and appreciate many of them, but often we aren't aware of the silent heroes that have contributed to our life as we know it.

The Road She Traveled is a project meant to honor and celebrate the women in our community that have changed not only the physical substance of the road we travel, but also the landscape we enjoy. Without the cherished contributions these women have made, we would work, live, and play in a very different community than the one encountered today.

We invite you to travel virtually down the road these remarkable women have paved and witness this gift to our community, a place for current and future history enthusiasts to learn about the unique and giving women who have helped to build this great city of La Crosse, Wisconsin!

With Admiration,

The Coulee Kids

Longfellow Middle School

La Crosse, Wisconsin

Source: Jeanne Halderson and Elizabeth Ramsay. *The Road She Traveled Project.* Accessed January 13, 2009, at http://www.sdlax.net/longfellow/theroadshetraveled/index.htm

Alternate site http://www.sdlax.net/longfellow/theroadshetraveled/behind_the_scenes/index.htm

On their site, visitors can also view an enhanced podcast (a podcast with images) about how the project evolved and who participates in it:

Figure 4.3

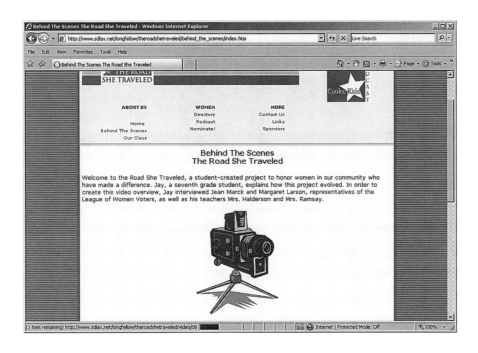

Source: Jeanne Halderson and Elizabeth Ramsay. *The Road She Traveled Project.* sdlax.net. Accessed January 27, 2009, at http://www.sdlax.net/longfellow/theroadshetraveled/behind_the_scenes/index.htm

Alternate site http://www.sdlax.net/longfellow/theroadshetraveled/behind_the_scenes/index.htm

As a connection to a book entitled *For the Common Good—A History of Women's Roles in LaCrosse County, 1920–1980,* the League of Women Voters approached members of the Longfellow Middle School faculty with the idea of documenting women's roles in the community around their school. The school purchased equipment such as scanners, cameras, and microphones with a grant from the League of Women Voters. They then sent out invitations to women across the county to come to the school to be interviewed. Teams of four students worked to create each podcast, with students taking turns being the interviewer, scanner, back-up interviewer, and the techie. In this way, each student had the opportunity to do some speaking and also use the technology.

In the first year of the project, 38 women participated in being interviewed. The school Web site currently boasts over 60 interviews of inspirational women—representing an impressive range of professions from government officials to businesswomen. The enhanced podcasts are posted on their Web site for all to enjoy:

Figure 4.4

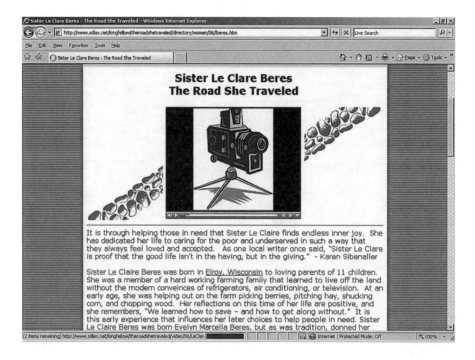

Source: Jeanne Halderson and Elizabeth Ramsay. *The Road She Traveled Project.* Accessed August 22, 2009, at http://www.sdlax.net/longfellow/theroadshetraveled/podcast/road.xml

Alternate site http://www.sdlax.net/longfellow/theroadshetraveled/behind_the_scenes/index.htm

This project exemplifies many of the 21st-century learning skills that we want our students to acquire during their K–12 experience. It is a means of raising the bar for students—as they are required to formulate ideas, write questions, speak confidently, and master the technical aspects of producing a podcast. The project also connects superbly to many TESOL standards and the TESOL technology standards. In the chart below, we can see ways in which the project connects to important standards on many levels.

"The Road She Traveled" Podcast Project: Standards Correlations

Students write invitations to women to participate in the project.		
21st-Century Skills	**TESOL Standards**	**TESOL Tech Standards**
• Critical Thinking and Problem-Solving Skills • Initiative and Self-Direction	• Goal 1, Standard 1: Students will use English to participate in social interactions.	• Goal 2: Students use technology in socially and culturally appropriate ways.

Students write invitations to women to participate in the project.		
21st-Century Skills	**TESOL Standards**	**TESOL Tech Standards**
• Social and Cross-Cultural Skills • Productivity and Accountability	• Goal 1, Standard 2: Students will interact in, through, and with spoken and written English for personal expression and enjoyment. • Goal 2, Standard 2: Students use English to obtain, process, construct, and provide subject matter information in spoken and written form.	

Students meet with the women, take digital photos, and interview them using digital recording equipment.		
21st-Century Skills	**TESOL Standards**	**TESOL Tech Standards**
• Critical Thinking and Problem-Solving Skills • Initiative and Self-Direction • Social and Cross-Cultural Skills • Communication and Collaboration Skills • Leadership and Responsibility	• Goal 1, Standard 1: Students will use English to participate in social interactions. • Goal 3, Standard 1: Students will use the appropriate language variety, register, and genre according to audience, purpose, and setting. • Goal 3, Standard 2: Students will use nonverbal communication appropriate to audience, purpose, and setting.	• Goal 2: Students use technology in socially and culturally appropriate ways.

Rules for Student Podcasting

Creating podcasts with students can be fun and exciting, but as with any other craft, there are basic rules of thumb for developing good podcasts. Here are a few suggestions adapted from Guidelines to Consider When Making ESL/EFL Podcasts by Charles Kelly:

General Guidelines for Any Podcast

Get the best possible sound quality.

- Get a good microphone.
- Record in a quiet place.
- Avoid recording in places with hard walls that give an echo.
- Avoid hum, hiss, computer fan noise and other distractions.
- Speaking close to the microphone often gives good results, but not so close that you get distortion or "pops" on letters like "P."
- Be careful to keep the recording level constant so the listener doesn't need to change the listening volume.

Additional Guidelines for ESL/EFL Podcasts

Make podcasts assuming that each show will be listened to more than once.

- ESL students are likely to want to relisten to the files.
- Keep them short, so they are easy to listen to more than once.
- Focus on one thing per show, so they make nice entries on play lists.

Don't include elements that interfere with understanding.

- Don't include background music under the talking.
- Don't include sound effects (or at least keep them to a bare minimum.)

Include the script (the text) of the podcast on the Web site.

- This allows students to easily look up words they don't understand.
- It may also allow students to use the material in ways that the podcaster might not have considered.
- Hearing impaired students can also benefit from your material.
- Search engines can help people find your podcasts.

Don't speak unnecessarily slowly.

- If you have included the script there is less of a need to speak slowly.
- While you don't want to speak too slowly, be careful to articulate each word, take breaths when appropriate, and accentuate and stress important words for or phrases for emphasis.
- It is acceptable to pause at natural phrase breaks a little longer than normal to allow students to digest the information, but pausing between each word leads to unnatural intonation and rhythm.

Make short podcasts.

- Think like a student. Which would you listen to first, a two-minute short lesson or a two-hour lecture?
- It's easier for the listener to commit himself or herself to a short amount of time.

Source: Adapted from Kelly, C. (2005). *Guidelines to Consider When Making ESL/EFL Podcasts.* Accessed August 14, 2009 at http://www.manythings.org/pod/guidelines.html

WHEN TO USE PODCASTS WITH ELL'S

Students at any age and proficiency level can participate in podcasting projects. Here are some suggestions for adapting the Coulee Kids' *The Road She Traveled* project for students in different grades.

Grades K–5

Community members could be interviewed by small groups of students together rather than individually. Younger students could interview the teacher and staff members in the school to start and then move on to invited guests such as parents and family members. The teacher could set up a class podcast in which several students' voices are heard on one podcast together.

Grades 6–8

Students can "interview" characters from literature that they are reading, scientists they are studying, and famous people in history. They can be asked to write a script that includes key points of information from any subject area, and then they should imagine what the interviewee's responses might be. For example, if they are learning about DNA, perhaps they could interview Watson and Crick—having one student conduct the interview by asking questions and two classmates taking the roles of Watson and Crick. Then, post the interview and ask classmates to post comments about the topics addressed in the conversations.

Grades 9–12

Have students design an investigative project in which they pose a problem or a question and then interview a series of people in their community about the topic. For example, students could ask about political issues (e.g., Do you agree with the immigration policies as they exist right now?) or cultural topics (e.g., What is your favorite book—and why?). They should be encouraged to edit their podcast and produce a segment for the class podcast library.

Podcasts have endless uses in the K–12 classroom. Whatever subject you teach—be it science or physical education—podcasting projects can be designed to connect to your discipline. Students feel motivated to share their work with a broad audience of listeners (and viewers, if doing an enhanced podcast) and enjoy sharing their own thoughts and opinions with the world at large.

WHO IS USING PODCASTS WITH ELL'S?

In this section, you will learn about educator Heather Tatton's analysis of ESLPod.com—an online source for podcasts for English language learners. Heather conducted action research by exploring the site and analyzing the strengths and weaknesses of the services. Finally, she offers her own perspective on what aspects are most beneficial for teaching ELLs.

An Analysis of ESL Pod

ESL Pod is a website that promotes listening, reading, and vocabulary skills for English Language Learners. I chose this site out of a desire to find appropriate listening texts to use with my current students. Many authentic sources like NPR, CNN, and others are too challenging; students struggle initially to semantically process the information and rarely progress beyond that in order to notice syntactic details. This is an issue of comprehensible input, or as Krashen would say, "i+1" (1985, p. 2); when students aren't able to comprehend overall meaning, the text is likely to contain structures way ahead of their current knowledge and is, therefore, not useful (Gass & Selinker, 2001). To compound this dilemma, the listening activities integrated with our course curriculum are too easy and are not representative of authentic language in use. Finding listening texts that are challenging and authentic, but not beyond the reach of the students has been problematic. ESL Pod appears to have achieved a middle ground. Their podcasts are reflective of authentic content, but with a slower pace of delivery, making their texts more accessible and comprehensible for ELLs. In addition, each podcast is accompanied by additional learning materials referred to as "learning guides."

The participants of ESL Pod include the designers, teachers, and ESL students. The site doesn't provide information about the technical developers or the people who maintain the website. However, information about the creators of the site is included. The masterminds behind ESL Pod are two ESL professors: Dr. Tse and Dr. McQuillan. According to the "About Us" information on the website, they volunteer to create and maintain the content and, between the two of them, do the recordings and materials development for all of the podcasts. Along with the people "behind the scenes," users of this website include teachers and students. All podcasts are free to download, but there is a charge for the learning guides. Themes are oriented toward adults or young adults and there is no difference between what a teacher downloads and what a student downloads (i.e. no teacher guides, additional explanations or activity instructions). Anyone can download podcasts, read the materials, answer the comprehension questions, and generally study the text independently and autonomously. For teachers, podcasts could be assigned as homework for their students or as a resource for group activities in the classroom.

Interactivity on ESL Pod is almost non-existent. Users have no ability to contribute to the site itself; they are merely passive receivers of the data. Nevertheless, the site does reflect a communicative approach in that the lessons are based on language in use rather than language structures and forms. By doing so, the site provides an open door to endless interactive and communicative learning opportunities in an offline setting. Users can download podcasts as well as the accompanying learning guides, all of which are intended to be used outside of the site (at home or in a classroom). In addition, users can transfer podcasts to their iPod, to iTunes, and to other listening software and/or portable devices. Thus, the site does provide numerous options for utilizing the listening texts. Teachers, for example, could be creating their own activities, above and beyond what is provided in the listening guides. ELLs may be sharing the podcasts with friends and having informal discussions or debates on the topics presented. The themes may inspire students to learn more and to do further research.

ESL Pod provides a service to ELLs and ESL/EFL teachers. Their listening texts and accompanying material reflect authentic language but at a reduced pace which makes them more accessible and useful for honing listening skills. It is a very useful tool for ELLs and teachers alike.

Source: Tatton, H. (2007, June 9). Heather's Tenor Analysis of ESL Pod. *StudyPlace.* Accessed August 9, 2009, at http://www.studyplace.org/wiki/Heather%27s_Tenor_Analysis_of_ESL_Pod

MAKE YOUR OWN PODCAST

Creating a podcast can be a fun but time-consuming project. There are many Web sites that help to make the process less complicated. PodOMatic is one popular choice for schools. MyPodcast, PodBean, and SwitchPod are all good options as well.

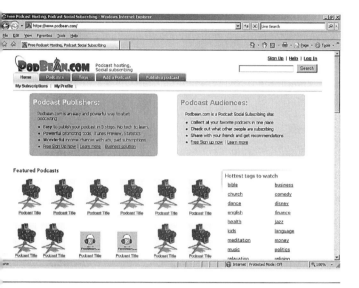

Source: PodBean.com

Source: PodOMatic.com

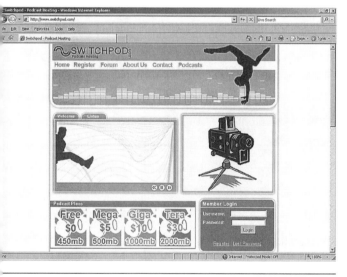

Source: SwitchPod.com

Source: MyPodcast.com

Each of these sites offers free blog hosting as well as step-by-step "wizards" that walk you screen-by-screen through the process of setting up a podcast. PodOMatic allows you to set up your own unique Web site URL (for example: http://www .schoolpodcast.podomatic.com/). The sites commonly offer a certain amount of storage space for free (PodOMatic gives you 500 MB of space), but then will charge for more space and more elaborate services. Most of these sites do post advertisements on your page that can be turned off for a fee.

It all starts by signing up for a free account. As with blogs and wikis, try to choose a username that is easy to remember. You will then be given the chance to create a unique URL. This name should reflect the group or class with which you will be working. For example: Period3ESL or AdvancedESLWriting. This will make the address easier for you and your students to remember and find later on. It will also make it easier for visitors to find what they are looking for in a Google or other search-engine search.

A podcast recording must first be created using a microphone and a digital recorder or your computer. The resulting mp3 file can then be uploaded into the podcast-hosting site. On PodOMatic, you can record directly onto the site by plugging a microphone into the computer jack and hitting the record button:

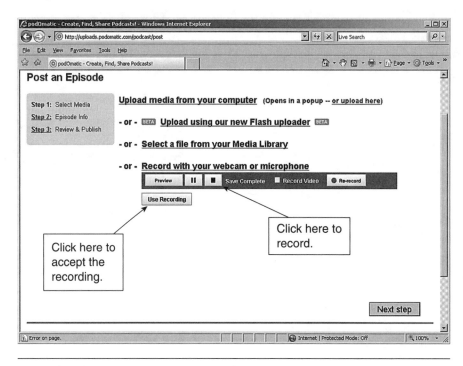

Source: PodOMatic.com. Accessed January 13, 2009, at http://uploads.podomatic.com/podcast/post

After recording, you can preview the clip. If you are satisfied with the way it sounds, click "use recording" and then hit "next step." Continue by writing a title and description for the podcast. The description should be short but also should contain words and phrases that would identify the contents of the podcast and help others to find it via a keyword search.

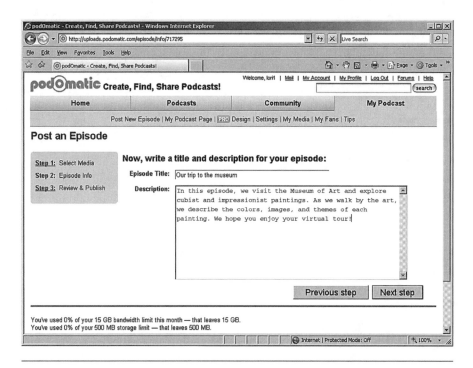

Source: PodOMatic.com. Accessed January 13, 2009, at http://uploads.podomatic.com/episode/info/

Click on "next step," and then add images if you like (this step is optional). Finally, add tags. As the Web site explains, "Tags are one word descriptions that make your episode more searchable." (PodOMatic.com). As with the description, tags allow others to find your podcast easily via a search engine.

Source: PodOMatic.com. Accessed January 13, 2009, at http://uploads.podomatic.com/episode/info/

To finish posting, click on the "post episode" button, and your podcast is ready to go! Share the URL (the Web site address) with your class, parents, administrators, and anyone who might be interested in hearing the voices of your English language learners!

● ● ●

WHERE TO FIND MORE INFORMATION ABOUT PODCASTS

REFERENCES

ESL Pod (n.d.). Retrieved June 3, 2007, from http://eslpodcast.com

Gardner, H. (1983). *Frames of mind.* NY: Basic Books.

Gass, S., & Selinker, L. (2001). *Second language acquisition: An introductory course.* New Jersey: Erlbaum Associates.

Krashen, S. (1985). *The input hypothesis: Issues and implications.* New York: Longman.

Tatton, H. (2007, June 9). Heather's tenor analysis of ESL pod. *StudyPlace.* Accessed August 09, 2009, at http://www.studyplace.org/wiki/Heather%27s_Tenor_Analysis_of_ESL_Pod

SUGGESTED READINGS

Borja, R. R. (2005, December 7). Podcasting craze comes to K–12 schools. *Education Week.* Retrieved August 15, 2009, from http://www.edweek.org/ew/articles/2005/12/07/14podcast.h25.html

Hendron, J. G., (2008). *RSS for educators: Blogs, newsfeeds, podcasts, and wikis in the classroom.* Eugene, OR: International Society for Technology in Education.

King, K. P., & Gura, M. (2008). *Podcasting for teachers—emerging technologies for evolving learners.* Charlotte, NC: Information Age.

Selingo, J. (2006, January 25). Students and teachers, from K–12, hit the podcasts. *New York Times.* Retrieved August 15, 2009, from http://www.nytimes.com/2006/01/25/technology/techspecia12/25podcast.html?_r=1&ex=1189742400&en=c2551319a7bbc9be&ei=5070

HELPFUL WEB SITES

English as a Second Language Podcasts—a good collection of podcasts on a variety of topics: http://a4esl.org/podcasts

ESLPod—a great collection of podcasts for students plus information for teachers about creating podcasts: http://www.eslpod.com

iTunes.com—there are hundreds of podcasts that are suitable for ELLs on iTunes (download for free at: http://www.apple.com/itunes/overview/), plus podcasts for educators on iTunes University: http://education.apple.com/itunesu

Radio WillowWeb—a series of student produced podcasts: http://www.mpsomaha.org/willow/radio/index.html

Teach Digital—curriculum by Wes Fryer: Podcasting: All you ever wanted to know about podcasting for teachers: http://teachdigital.pbwiki.com/podcasting

The Why's and How's of ESL Classroom Podcasting—view an excellent slideshow with a rationale regarding poscasting with ELLs: http://www.slideshare.net/shjduarte/esl-classroom-podcasting

5

Viewing, Creating, and Sharing Video

YouTube and TeacherTube

> **Video connection:** Prior to reading this chapter, view the online video "What is YouTube?" at http://www.youtube.com/watch?v=aHznRSydPxw

WHAT ARE YOUTUBE AND TEACHERTUBE?

Online video hosts allow users to upload personal videos and store them on a "channel" for others to view, comment on, rate, and share with friends. In this chapter, we will explore two different Web 2.0 tools that involve students not just watching videos online but also in creating and posting their own video productions.

Perhaps the most famous (and sometimes *infamous*) online video host site is YouTube. Put simply, YouTube is a Web site that allows registered users to upload and share digital videos. Users create their own channel and house their videos on this page. Viewers can comment on videos, add them to playlists, subscribe to others' channels, rate videos, and become "friends" with other registered users.

📄 **YOUTUBE**

With people viewing "hundreds of millions of videos a day on YouTube," it is no wonder that our students have become very familiar with this Web site. According to the YouTube Web site, the

> user base is broad in age range, 18–55, evenly divided between males and females, and spanning all geographies. Fifty-one percent of . . . users go to YouTube weekly or more often, and 52 percent of 18–34 year-olds share videos often with friends and colleagues. (YouTube, accessed August 15, 2009, at http://www.youtube.com/t/fact_sheet)

Notice that the ages listed in these statistics begin at age 18. Technically, users should be 18 years old to open an account to upload videos on YouTube. Furthermore, according to YouTube, "the YouTube website is not intended for children under 13" (accessed on May 12, 2009, at www.youtube.com/t/terms). As YouTube contains videos that can be risqué (or worse), many schools—and sometimes even entire countries—choose to block it (as has been the case at various times in Thailand, Turkey, China, and Kuwait). When using YouTube videos with students, it is helpful to download or capture the video prior to class so that access is guaranteed and there is no risk of students finding videos that are other than educational. For this reason, it is also important to address critical viewing and media literacy issues with students so that they are prepared when they stumble across video segments that are not meant for the eyes of young viewers.

Despite the need for some caution, YouTube and other video-sharing sites are some of the most useful tools available for teaching English. Videos for grammar, vocabulary, and pronunciation practice abound. Videos that cover an almost endless variety of content areas (from architecture to zoology) can be found with a few computer key clicks. Videos that connect students to other English language learners around the world abound on YouTube. And these are just the ways in which students can passively use video-sharing sites (i.e., by viewing and listening). When used as a means of creating, posting, and sharing student-created videos, YouTube becomes a means of fostering creativity in students as well as a powerful tool for active speaking practice. It can inspire students to become filmmakers, actors, and script writers. They take on the role of digital storytellers—and they use English to tell their stories. To sum it up, the benefits of using YouTube with ELLs far outweigh the caution needed to use this tool.

Components of YouTube and TeacherTube

The video-sharing sites YouTube and TeacherTube can be searched and viewed without having an account. There is a search box on the homepage of both sites that allows you to type in some key words and phrases to narrow your search:

Figure 5.1

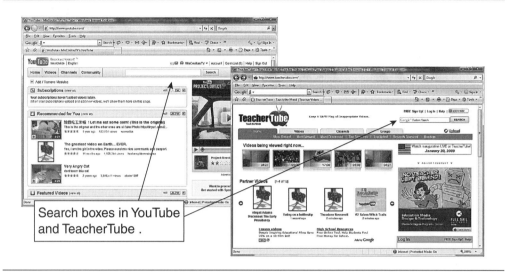

Search boxes in YouTube and TeacherTube .

Source: YouTube.com and TeacherTube.com

For adult users interested in signing up for a free account in order to upload videos, a channel is created that will bear a unique URL (Web address). For example, this language-learning channel is called MisCositasTV and can be accessed online at: www.youtube.com/user/miscositastv. Users with a channel on YouTube can edit their channel, upload videos, create playlists, and invite friends to view their videos. Viewers who like the channel can subscribe. An e-mail notification will be sent to subscribers each time a new video is uploaded.

Figure 5.2

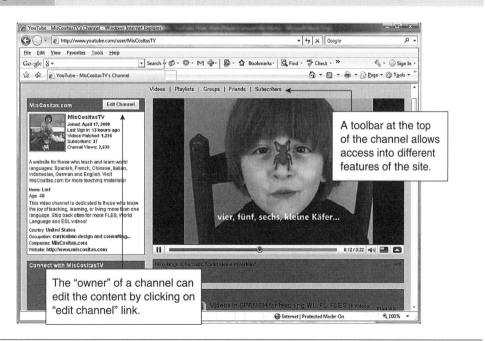

A toolbar at the top of the channel allows access into different features of the site.

The "owner" of a channel can edit the content by clicking on "edit channel" link.

Source: YouTube.com. Accessed January 19, 2009, at www.youtube.com/user/MiscositasTV

Commenting on YouTube and TeacherTube

YouTube and TeacherTube allow the same sorts of comments as do blogs: linear text or video comments that are listed chronologically below a post (in this case, below the video).

Figure 5.3

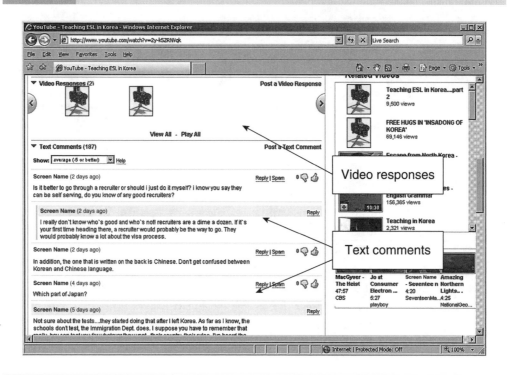

Source: YouTube.com. Accessed on January 19, 2009, at http://www.youtube.com/watch?v=2y-k5ZRNVqk

Commenting on videos is fun and motivational for students. Receiving comments on their own productions can be even more exciting as their work is viewed by an online global community. Furthermore, the act of leaving and receiving comments can be a good opportunity for students to discuss the proper language with which to leave constructive criticism as well as politeness norms.

WHY VIEW, CREATE, AND SHARE VIDEOS WITH ELL'S?

YouTube, a fantastic source for English-language-learning videos, is a useful forum in which to share student-created videos. As we have seen with podcasts, ELL students are often hesitant to perform, do skits, or otherwise speak in front of their fellow students. If given the option to create a video of their work, students often feel more in control and more at ease because they can record, rerecord, and edit their presentation prior to sharing it with the class. They can also add subtitles, effects, and other features that both enhance the visual presentation and extend the language-learning aspect of the project. For example, here is a skit produced by English language learners in Korea:

Figure 5.4

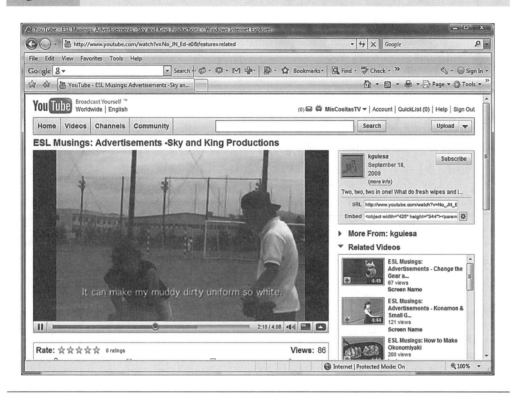

Source: YouTube.com. Accessed on August 9, 2009, at http://www.youtube.com/watch?v=No_JN_Ed-e0

In this video, subtitles support comprehension for those watching the video. They also serve to extend the activity for students creating the video because they were required to listen to their audio script several times in order to type in the correct subtitles for their video.

Videos allow students to make decisions about the images they include in their presentation, background music, titles, and other details. It is a complete creative process with ample differentiation of tasks to connect with a variety of different learning styles: Visual learners can design imagery, costumes, and choose colors; auditory learners can work with the dialogue, music, and sound effects; and tactile/kinesthetic learners can design

Quick List

Use online videos for . . .

- Documenting and filming student classroom presentations
- Movie or TV-show parodies
- Screencasts (a movie of changes that occur on a computer monitor, often used for training and educational purposes)
- PhotoStory movies
- Film and book reviews
- Acting out plays or literature
- Cooking shows
- Science demonstrations
- Music videos

sets and manipulate the images by ordering and sequencing them in the project.

Finally, as we have seen with other Web 2.0 tools, creating and sharing videos with students is not just pedagogically sound but also fun and motivational for students. If you were to take a poll of your students, you would likely find that most of them have visited YouTube for viewing purposes and that many of them have actually created and posted their own videos. Many students *love* to see themselves on camera and will often work harder on a videotaped project than on one that is simply to be presented "live" in class.

HOW TO USE YOUTUBE AND TEACHERTUBE WITH ELL'S: SAMPLE YOUTUBE ACTIVITIES

Students can be both "users" of videos on YouTube and "producers," by making their own videos to post on their channel. What follow are some ideas for using YouTube with ELLs along with some existing video channels that have collections of videos that are of particular use in the ESL classroom.

Most of us start our "YouTube in the classroom experience" as consumers of videos. We search for videos that cover vocabulary, grammar, or content goals that we have in our own lesson plans. Some YouTube channels that provide consistently good videos for ELLs are

- **Podenglish:** Produced by EF English, the slogan is "watch, learn, try," and the segments are humorous. Here's a link called "Office Talk." It has short questions and short answers. Good for stop-and-repeat practice: www.YouTube.com/watch?v=wnZJpPM9YxM
- **Jenniferesl:** Good production on a tripod. Example: In/on grammar, www.YouTube.com/watch?v=GinSHimulAo
- **Sozoexchange:** From sozoexchange.com, the video series presents a daily word. Example: "Equivalent," www.youtube.com/watch?v=GmR_IW4KQ1U

Unfortunately, though, there are some schools that block YouTube and similar video-sharing sites. In this case, you can download videos from YouTube, record them on DVD or CD, and bring them into your school. Here's one way that it works.

1. Go to http://www.downloadyoutubevideo.org

2. Copy the link of the YouTube video that you want to download.

3. Paste the link in the box shown on the page.

After the file is downloaded onto your hard drive, you need to have a Flash video (FLV) player on your computer (http://www.flash2x .net/flashplayer/), or you can go another step to convert the file. The file will be called "get_video." You need to rename the file as "get_video.flv" (add ".flv" to the name). Then, you can download the converter software.

You can get the converter at http://applian.com/replay-converter/ demo.php. You can try the program at no charge. The demo is fully functional, except for a watermark added to videos. To see what a conversion looks like, you can go to "freeenglishlessons" and look for the converted file called "equivalent." Replay Converter turns FLV video files (captured from YouTube and other video sites) and turns them into popular formats: DVD discs, iPod video, wmv, avi, mpeg-4, mp3, and 3gp (for mobile phones).

Once we find great videos, there are different ways we can incorporate them into our teaching in the ESL classroom. Here are some examples:

- Teachers can identify videos that will help students practice grammar or vocabulary that were presented in class. Teachers can e-mail links to each student.
- Teachers can post YouTube links to a teacher Web site or blog, and students can click on the links for practice.
- YouTube can be used as a media library. Teachers can collect links for dictations, "new vocabulary" videos, conversation practice, pronunciation practice, and grammar review.
- Teachers can assign homework. (Imagine: A teacher can video record the homework assignment and post it to YouTube, and students can watch the instructions!) Here is an example of a homework assignment called "Vocabulary for Cars": www.youtube.com/watch? v=2WoIBwqZyFQ

Finally, once teachers and students become comfortable with YouTube, students can create and post their own videos. For example, students can write a script, perform a scene from a story or a play, and post their video. Classmates can be asked to post text or video reviews, comments, or suggestions relating to their classmates' video. Here are some tips for creating the best quality videos possible:

- **Be consistent in quality.** Check the acoustics. Make sure there are no traffic sounds in the background. Check the quality of the sound (sometimes the volume is too low or distorted by a bad microphone). Use a tripod, if possible, for a steady shot.
- **Be consistent in titles.** Have a look at the YouTube channel Podenglish. There are 58 videos, all with a similar format (e.g., "Learn English 10"). This type of numbering system is very convenient for users.
- **Use clear tags.** If it's a pronunciation video, be sure to include "pronunciation" as one of the tags, not just "English practice."

- **Use subtitles.** Put more words on the screen. This is helpful for students who are visual learners and might need to see a word to be able to understand it better.

Source: Used with permission from Steve McCrea. FreeEnglishLessons.com

It is almost inevitable that the first few videos you make will be choppy, poorly edited, or hard to hear. As you become experienced using editing software, holding the camera, and setting up shots, your videos will improve dramatically. See the "Make Your Own Video" section later in this chapter for a description of MovieMaker editing software. It's not hard to use; it just takes practice, patience, and someone to guide you through the process.

"ELLs as Users and Producers on YouTube": Standards Correlations

Students create a storyboard or write a script to accompany the plot of their video.		
21st-Century Skills	**TESOL Standards**	**TESOL Tech Standards**
• Creativity and Innovation Skills • Critical Thinking and Problem-Solving Skills • Communication and Collaboration Skills • Media Literacy • Productivity and Accountability • Leadership and Responsibility	• Goal 2, Standard 2: Students use English to obtain, process, construct, and provide subject matter information in spoken and written forms. • Goal 2, Standard 3: Students will use appropriate learning strategies to construct and apply academic knowledge.	• Goal 2: Students use technology in socially and culturally appropriate ways. • Goal 3: Students use technology-based tools as aids in the development of their language-learning competence as part of formal instruction and for further learning.

Students perform a skit for a YouTube video.		
21st-Century Skills	**TESOL Standards**	**TESOL Tech Standards**
• Communication and Collaboration Skills • Social and Cross-Cultural Skills • Information, Media, and Technology Skills	• Goal 3, Standard 1: Students will use the appropriate language variety, register, and genre according to audience, purpose, and setting.	• Goal 2: Students use technology in socially and culturally appropriate ways. • Goal 3: Students use technology-based tools as aids in the

Students perform a skit for a YouTube video.		
21st-Century Skills	**TESOL Standards**	**TESOL Tech Standards**
• Productivity and Accountability	• Goal 3, Standard 2: Students will use nonverbal communication appropriate to audience, purpose, and setting.	development of their language-learning competence as part of formal instruction and for further learning.

Students respond to others' video posts through text, audio, or video comments.		
21st-Century Skills	**TESOL Standards**	**TESOL Tech Standards**
• Critical Thinking and Problem-Solving Skills • Information, Media, and Technology Skills • Initiative and Self-Direction • Social and Cross-Cultural Skills	• Goal 1, Standard 1: Students will interact in, through, and with spoken and written English for personal expression and enjoyment.	• Goal 2: Students use technology in socially and culturally appropriate ways.

Guidelines for Using YouTube and TeacherTube in the Classroom

Creating videos for YouTube or TeacherTube can be fun, but it is important to talk to students about ways in which to be safe in using this powerful Web 2.0 tool. Here are the "Top 10 Safety Tips for Video-Sharing" from ConnectSafely.org (2008). It is helpful to go over these recommendations with students and parents before student work is posted to a video-sharing Web site:

1. **Tough to take back**. Whatever you post is basically permanent. Even if you later delete it, there is a chance that it has been copied, forwarded, or reposted. And there are Web archives that hang on to content even after it has been taken down.

2. **What the background reveals**. Think about what's in the scene you're recording: posters on your wall, photos on a shelf, school or team t-shirts people are wearing, address signs in front of a house or car license-plate numbers all can reveal your identity or location. What you say during recording can too.

(Continued)

(Continued)

3. **'You are what you wear.'** It's an old maxim with new meaning in online video. Think about what your appearance "says" about you. Would you feel comfortable showing this video to your boss or potential employer, a relative, or your future mother- or father-in-law?

4. **Respecting others' privacy**. Be respectful of the privacy rights of people in your video. If taping in a public place, be sure to ask permission before including bystanders, and never take video of children without their parents' permission.

5. **Everybody's a videographer**. Don't think someone needs a videocam to record video. Most cell phones and still cameras are also now video recorders. Be aware that when people take out a cell phone, they could be using it as a camera or camcorder.

6. **Be a good citizen**. It's your right to express your point of view and even make fun of public officials or policies, but don't be mean or nasty, especially when it comes to people who aren't in the public eye. You can be held legally responsible if you slander, libel, or defame someone.

7. **Respect terms of use**. Most video sites have terms of service that you must adhere to. Most of them prohibit sexually explicit content, gratuitous violence, and videos that are harassing, defamatory, obscene, libelous, hateful, or violating other people's privacy. Most responsible sites report videos depicting child exploitation and threatening or illegal acts.

8. **Respect copyrights.** All reputable video-sharing sites prohibit the unauthorized use of copyrighted material. Of course that means that you can't rip-off segments from TV shows or movies. But it also means: Think about the music tracks you use in videos.

9. **Talk with kids about video bullying**. Creating a video that makes fun of or ridicules another person can be extremely hurtful. This and other forms of cyberbullying are a growing problem on the Internet which affects many children and teens.

10. **Kids' Web video viewing**. As with all media, parental discretion is not only advised—it's a necessary part of parenting. Even though most of the major sites prohibit pornography and gratuitous violence, there are videos that are not suitable for younger children and there are some sites that do permit video that may be inappropriate for children or teens.

Source: Used with permission from Anne Collier. ConnectSafely.org. Accessed August 16, 2009, at http://www.connectsafely.org/Safety-Tips/top-10-safety-tips-for-video-sharing.html

WHEN TO USE YOUTUBE OR TEACHERTUBE WITH ELL'S

YouTube is a site that does not discriminate among its users. If you use the right (or wrong!) search terms, a user is just as likely to pull up a video meant for adults as he is to find ones that are "rated G." For this reason, when sending students—especially younger ones—to YouTube, it is important to monitor them closely.

Grades K–5

Have elementary students interview family members or people in school. Edit the clips together to create a class video. Students can also create a video response to their favorite picturebook or storytime character. They can connect to other classrooms around the world by sharing video or photos as in iEarn's Teddy Bear Project (http://www.iearn.org.au/tbear/).

Grades 6–8

Middle schoolers can design and film public service announcements about issues in their school or community. They can create skits about adolescent issues such as bullying, cliques, or fairness and share these with other classes. They can also write, design, edit, and film a video tour of their school for newcomers. This student-created video could be shown to new ESL students and their parents in September. Students might also be asked to create a "how to" video about something of importance to them. For example, they could teach their home language or show viewers how to cook or play a musical instrument. To practice speaking and pronunciation, students should narrate the steps to their "how to" project.

Grades 9–12

Videos can be created by high school students for any class. Students can re-create historical events as a means of studying for a history exam or present a virtual art show featuring photographs of their paintings, sculptures, or designs. They can record or photograph lab experiments and create a video lab report. Students can write their autobiography and share their narratives through a dramatic video presenting the stories of their lives.

There is no limit to the possibilities that creating and sharing videos offers to the ESL teacher and ELLs in general. There are already many examples online that show projects from ESL students from around the world. Our students can view these projects as exemplars and then create their own as a means of sharing their knowledge, their feelings, and their ideas through imagery and sound—all while also practicing their English for an authentic audience.

WHO IS USING YOUTUBE AND TEACHERTUBE WITH ELL'S?

In the following story, the author of the blog EFL Geek (located online http://eflgeek.com/) shares his thought processes as he becomes inspired to use more videos with his ELLs—and ultimately to make even better ones. He shares some of his ideas about creating online videos for English language learners as well as some tips for video hosting sites other than YouTube.

LIGHTS, CAMERA, ACTION!

As an English teacher in Korea, the author of the blog EFLGeek has been exploring the use of online videos with his students. As most of us do, he started to use videos by simply showing them to students to illustrate a point or topic of discussion. For example, he found two videos on YouTube from the language learning company Berlitz highlight the importance of knowing more than one language:

- *German Coast Guard commercial: http://www.youtube.com/watch?v=gmOTpIVxji8*
- *Cat vs. Mouse commercial: http://eflgeek.com/index.php/eflgeek/comments/another-english-commercial*

Further investigation of YouTube yielded many more useful videos for teaching ESL or EFL. These include one from a teacher in Japan that contains tongue twisters and pronunciation exercises: the Daily English Show (http://youtube.com/profile? user=thedailyenglishshow)

After sharing videos with students, the teacher moved on to incorporate the videos with a script. In other words, students could watch the video while at the same time reading the words that were being spoken. In his blog, the teacher reflects on his rationale for including the script: " I realize that the video may be a little complex for many students, but I posted the script to my site and the context of the page should help as well."

YouTube, TeacherTube and other video sharing sites proved to be an excellent source of authentic (and short) listening and viewing material for these EFL students. In order to make sure that videos were always available to him (and in case the Internet goes down in the middle of a lesson), EFLGeek uploads videos to his student webpage. This ensures that the videos are working properly each time he or a student wants to access them.

Once students were comfortable viewing videos, it was time to encourage them to create movie and video reviews. EFLGeek gave students specific guidelines and asked them to film themselves reviewing a clip. The resulting video was shown in his classes. This not only provided students with an authentic task, but also with an authentic audience of viewers – their classmates and friends.

Moving on from reviews, the teacher began to explore filmmaking with his students. He felt that he and his own students could create better videos than many of those that are currently available on YouTube. The teacher and class have designed a proposal to get funding from their school for high-quality video cameras and sound equipment. In the meanwhile, however, EFLGeek and his class have all that is needed to produce a video for YouTube: a digital video camera and an Internet connection. The class plans to create a library of videos and DVDs to be used in class, for enrichment, or self-study, and homework.

In his exploration of online videos, the teacher/blogger EFL Geek moved from simply viewing videos to creating videos in the following order:

1. *viewing videos*
2. *viewing videos with integrated scripts*

3. reviewing videos
4. creating videos

Videos have many uses in the ESL/EFL classroom. Choose the one that best suits your school context!

Paraphrased from http://eflgeek.com/index.php/eflgeek/comments/you-tube-and-esl/

MAKE YOUR OWN VIDEO

There are many sites to choose from that allow users to search for and host videos. The most popular are YouTube and TeacherTube. Other educational video-sharing Web sites are SchoolTube and KidsTube.

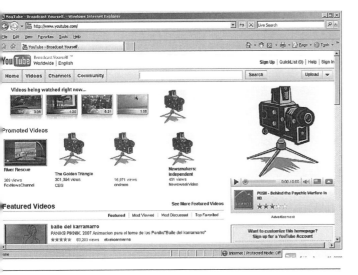

Source: YouTube.com

Source: TeacherTube.com

Source: SchoolTube.com

Source: KidsTube.com

Filming a video and posting it to YouTube is easy. Editing a video so that it has smooth transitions and features that support language learning requires another step. Most all Windows computers have a free movie editing program called Windows MovieMaker (if you can't find it on your computer, click on the start menu and do a search for it by name). This program is a quick and easy way to edit still or video images into a polished looking movie—ready for uploading to YouTube or for sharing with your class.

After opening the program, the first step is importing images or video clips.

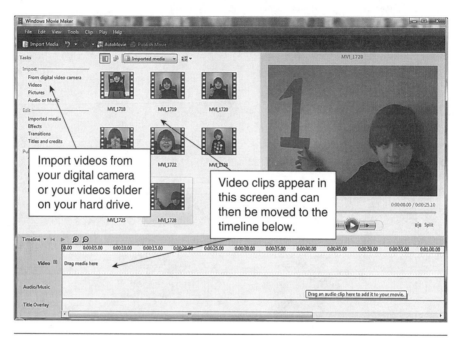

Source: Windows MovieMaker

Once all the clips are imported into the program, they can be edited by dragging on the clip at the front or back to cut unwanted scenes. The clip can also be split into two sections to facilitate editing or to delete an entire section.

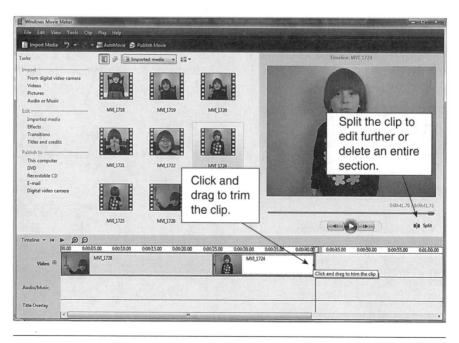

Source: Windows MovieMaker

Titles and credits can be added at the beginning of the movie, before the selected clip, on the selected clip, or at the end as credits. The program also allows users to change the color and style of the titles to suit the mood or message of the movie.

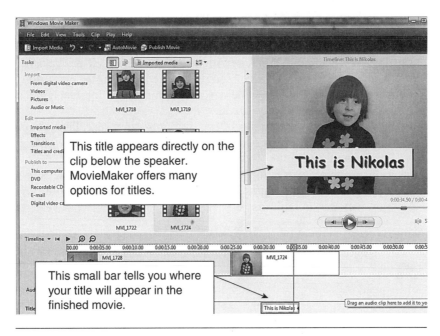

Source: Windows MovieMaker

Once you are satisfied with the video, look for the "Publish to" toolbar and then decide on the format. It is often best to publish to a particular computer and then save the file before sending it via e-mail or burning it to a DVD. Give the movie a name, click through the next screen, and click on "publish." Your movie will be transformed into a .wmv (Windows Media Video) file that can be played on any Windows machine.

● ● ●

WHERE TO FIND MORE INFORMATION ABOUT YOUTUBE AND TEACHERTUBE

SUGGESTED READINGS

Jakes, D. (2005, December 1). Making the case for digital storytelling. *Tech & Learning.* Retrieved August 16, 2009, from http://www.techlearning.com/article/4958
Underdahl, M. (2000). *Microsoft Windows MovieMaker for dummies.* NY: Hungry Minds.

HELPFUL WEB SITES

The ESL Movies Project—ESL students create a news broadcast—lesson plans and instructions for teachers who want to create videos with their ELLs: http://sites.google.com/site/eslmoviesproject

For Mac users, an iMovie tutorial: http://www.youtube.com/watch?v=3EXan Bq68mI

High School Students: Why You Must Display Caution When Using YouTube. *ESL Teachers' Board*—a brief article with good advice for students: http://www .eslteachersboard.com/cgi-bin/website/index.pl?read=444

Jakes Online—resources for digital literacy such as lessons, links, and activities: http://www.jakesonline.org/visual.htm

Making an Educational YouTube video—an article and video clip with suggestions from an ESL teacher: http://englishbabyblog.com/tag/youtube

PhotoStory tutorial—an excellent screencast tutorial for teachers: http://www .jakesonline.org/photostory.htm

Using YouTube for Vocabulary Development—some excellent suggestions from an ESL teacher: http://eltnotebook.blogspot.com/2007/07/using-youtube-for-vocabulary.html

Windows MovieMaker tutorials—this tutorial will take you step-by-step through the MovieMaker program: http://www.microsoft.com/windowsxp/using/ moviemaker/default.mspx

6

Sharing Visual Media

VoiceThread and Flickr

Video connection: Prior to reading this chapter, view the online video "Online Photo Sharing in Plain English" at http://www.commoncraft.com/photosharing

WHAT IS VISUAL MEDIA?

Beginning with still images, photo sharing Web sites proliferate on the World Wide Web. Web sites like KodakGallery.com, Shutterfly.com, and Snapfish.com all provide users with free space on which to house and share digital photos. On these sites, users can store digital images, print them out, and even order high quality hard copies of photos via the online platform. Flickr.com provides all of these services for users, but also allows for the establishment of groups so that people with like interests can share their photos easily. Flickr is yet another social networking site (like Facebook and MySpace), but it is based around the digital photographic image.

 FLICKR

The benefits of a site like Flickr are described on its homepage:

We want to enable new ways of organizing photos and video. Once you make the switch to digital, it is all too easy to get overwhelmed with the sheer number of photos you take or videos you shoot with that itchy trigger finger. Albums, the principal way people go about organizing things today, are great–until you get to 20 or 30 or 50 of them. They worked in the days of getting rolls of film developed, but the "album" metaphor is in desperate need of a Florida condo and full retirement.

Part of the solution is to make the process of organizing photos or videos collaborative. In Flickr, you can give your friends, family, and other contacts permission to organize your stuff—not just to add comments, but also notes and tags. People like to ooh and ahh, laugh and cry, make wisecracks when sharing photos and videos. Why not give them the ability to do this when they look at them over the Internet? And as all this info accretes as metadata, you can find things so much easier later on, since all this info is also searchable.

Source: Accessed August 16, 2009, at http://www.flickr.com/about/

Thus, Flickr is a site that allows for users to easily upload and organize digital images and share them with others, who can comment, rate, and save the photos for themselves.

Another site that facilitates the sharing of digital images is VoiceThread. According to the Web site, VoiceThread is particularly effective in education in that

a VoiceThread allows every child in a class to record audio commentary about the ideas and experiences that are important to them. Whether an event, a project, or a milestone, children can tell their story in their own voice, and then share it with the world.

For teachers, VoiceThreads offer a single vessel to capture and then share all the diverse personalities of an entire class. You will hear the pride and excitement in their voices as the students "publish" their work. A VoiceThread can be managed with little effort, creating an heirloom that can be shared by students, parents, and educators alike.

Source: Accessed on August 16, 2009, at http://voicethread.com/classroom.php

VoiceThread and Flickr are similar in that the programs allow for easy uploading of images, and they give viewers the ability to comment. While Flickr's interface allows for a linear commenting environment (much like on a blog, the comments are listed one after the other underneath a particular photo), VoiceThread comments appear alongside the main image, and can be text, voice, or video comments. VoiceThread has a global following, and people from around the world can create projects and participate in activities created by other members.

Components of VoiceThread and Flickr

Flickr makes it easy to upload and organize visual media. Once you have some photos in your "photostream" (your photo collection), there are tabs that allow users to organize files, send links and photos to contacts, view groups, or explore other people's collections.

Figure 6.1

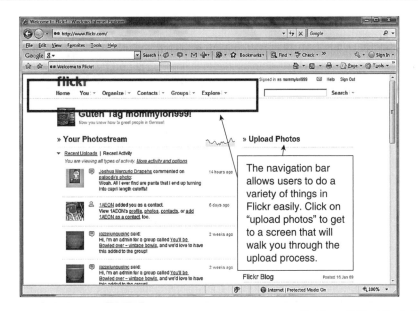

Source: Accessed August 16, 2009, at www.flickr.com

By clicking on the groups tab, users can search for, view, and even join groups of interest to them.

Figure 6.2

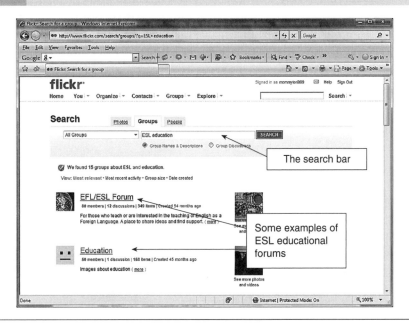

Source: Accessed August 16, 2009, at www.flickr.com/search/groups

VoiceThread is a site that is visually appealing and fun to use. After setting up an account, users can upload images, arrange them as they like, and create comments. Once a user creates and posts a VoiceThread, they are kept in the "dashboard," a sort of organizer, that can be reached by clicking on the "MyVoice" tab:

Figure 6.3

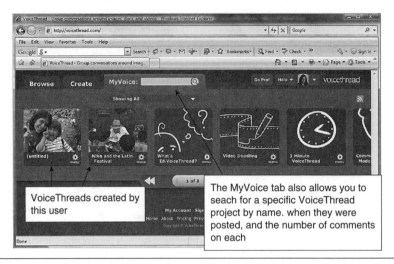

Source: Accessed August 16, 2009, at www.voicethread.com

Commenting on VoiceThread and Flickr

Part of the fun of these sites is not just the ability to share visual media with others but to send and receive comments on the media—often times in very direct ways. On Flickr, for example, along with the traditional comment section that appears below a particular image and runs chronologically (i.e., one comment after another according to date posted), users can also comment directly onto a photo in a format called "notes." A small box can be drawn around a particular section of the photo and text can be added to comment on that particular feature. Below is a good example using a photo of a student's hand. Each box represents a different comment. When a viewer moves the mouse over each box, the comments appear next to the boxes along with the name of the commentor.

Figure 6.4

Source: Accessed August 16, 2009, at http://www.flickr.com/photos/aisforangie/16186751

This feature allows for more specific comments that interact directly with the visual image. As the byline on the Web site states, VoiceThread facilitates "Group conversations around images." Thus, on VoiceThread, comments are the *raison d'etre* of the site. The comments can be in text, voice, or video format:

Figure 6.5

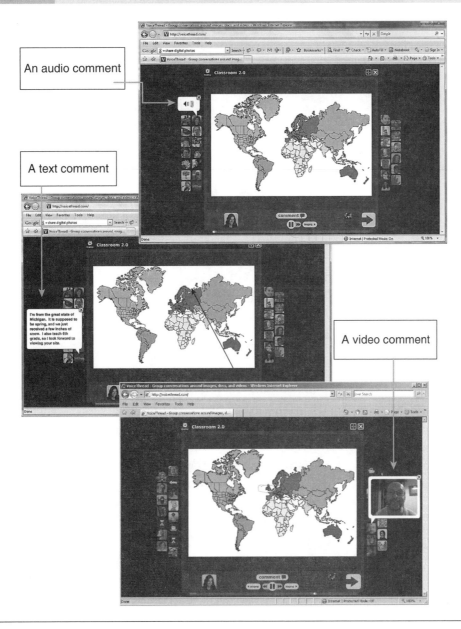

Source: Accessed August 16, 2009, at www.voicethread.com

The comments flank the image and, as is the case with Flickr notes, viewers can interact directly with the image. In this VoiceThread, users add comments about their home country while also circling their homes on the map with a virtual pen:

Figure 6.6

Source: Accessed on August 16, 2009, at www.voicethread.com

WHY CREATE AND SHARE VISUAL MEDIA WITH ELL'S?

One of the central—and most effective—strategies in working with English language learners is the use of visuals to scaffold comprehension. In teaching everything from vocabulary and grammatical structures to culture and content, images—still or moving—help ELLs to better understand information. Visual media online provides teachers of ELLs with an almost infinite number of sources for images. For example, a simple Google image search (www.images.google.com) yields an almost limitless supply of photos, illustrations, and diagrams on any topic that can be tremendously helpful in the ESL classroom.

But as we have seen with Web 2.0 technologies like blogs and podcasts, accessing material that has been created by others is half the fun—and yields only a portion of the educational benefits. The true benefit to ELLs comes when they are in control of and responsible for creating imagery and sharing it online. A good example of such a student-directed project would be the traditional picture dictionary. We have often asked younger or beginning students to cut and paste pictures from magazines in order to create a picture dictionary or glossary. With online sources of images—and Web sites that facilitate housing and sharing the "dictionaries" like Flickr or VoiceThread—students can create more dynamic and useful products, share them with classmates online, and even with other English language learners around the world. Two examples of such online projects include a cultural poster and an art-based project. This cultural project involves students in creating a poster, uploading a digitized version of Flickr, and eliciting classmates' comments:

Figure 6.7

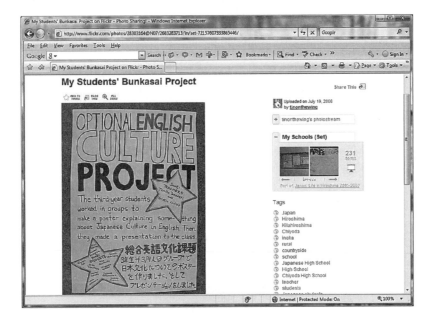

Source: Accessed January 18, 2009, at http://www.flickr.com/photos/28303164@N07/2683283713/in/set-72157607333865446

For another project, the teacher uploaded images of Colombian artist Fernando Botero's paintings to elicit student's descriptions using prepositional phrases:

Figure 6.8

Source: Accessed August 16, 2009, at http://voicethread.com/share/61467

Both of these projects included some use of imagery to elicit English language production—either in writing or via oral comments. They extended the traditional classroom-based activity by providing students with an authentic context for communicating their thoughts and ideas.

Both Flickr and YouTube have collections of images that are available for public commenting. In Flickr, an area called "The Commons" (www.flickr.com/commons) is one example of an online photo repository:

Figure 6.9

Source: Accessed August 16, 2009, at http://www.flickr.com/commons

This area contains a large collection of images from public photography archives. Visitors are invited to view and comment on the photos that include images from the collections of the Smithsonian, the Library of Congress, and the New York Public Library. Also housed in the collections are images from public or national libraries from around the world, such as those of New Zealand, France, Australia, and Scotland.

Students can collect visual media projects during their tenure in an ESL program to document their progress over time. By building a "virtual portfolio" with text, audio, and video files, students, parents, teachers, and administrators can readily see language progress, as well as marvel in the physical changes that a typical child goes through during a school year. At the end of the year, teachers can ask students to comment on their own photos, VoiceThreads,

---

Quick List

Use media sharing sites for . . .

- Virtual tours of different towns, states, countries, and important sites around the world
- A "What is it?" game with students guessing uses for an uncommon object
- Autobiographies
- Geography studies
- Visual representations of novels, stories, and picture books
- Evidence to support an argument using visual data or primary sources
- Debates on a topic or essential question

or videos as a means of including a self-reflection component to the portfolio. By adding a rubric and assessing the portfolio at the end of the school year, teachers will have a pre-postprogram assessment that is both valid and enjoyable to watch.

HOW TO USE VOICETHREAD AND FLICKR WITH ELL'S: DIGITAL STORYTELLING WITH VOICETHREAD

One of the key components of VoiceThread is the possibility of inviting moderated audio or written commentary on the work created. Other children can leave audio or text comments on a piece of digital work, and you, as their teacher, can choose to allow it or not. It is incredible that children can interact with each other via the Web through the sound of their voice. How powerful is that as a way to create a sense of audience?

There are many more VoiceThreads available online, spanning a variety of media genres including poetry, self-portraits, lectures, book reviews, multimedia presentations, and digital stories. Why not add your students' work to the mix? For example, consider the following VoiceThread projects:

- **Poem book:** In this activity, participants share their favorite poems to create an audio poem book. ELLs create their book by adding their audio narration and then sharing the work online. View online at http://voicethread.com/view.php?b=579
- **Great book stories:** According to Wes Fryer (SpeedofCreativity.org), the idea is basic: Narrate five pictures to share why you love a specific book, and why other people should read it. If you're interested in contributing, please check out the site and the guidelines. The password to edit the wiki is *share*. View online at http://greatbook stories.pbwiki.com
- **Social studies and geography applications:** This VoiceThread has users leaving comments on maps from around the world. View online at http://voicethread.com/view.php?b=971
- **Teaching chemistry lecture:** No, digital creations aren't just for elementary school students! View online at http://voicethread.com/view.php?b=5941
- **A student presentation:** *The Invisible Children* http://voicethread.com/view.php?b=5087

Source: Miguel Guehlin

"Digital storytelling begins," says Joe Lambert, cofounder of the Center for Digital Storytelling, "with the notion that in the not [too] distant future, sharing one's story through the multiple mediums of digital imagery, text, voice, sound, music, video and animation will be THE PRINCIPAL HOBBY OF THE WORLD'S PEOPLE" (quoted in Fryer, 2007).

As that world becomes more connected through the Internet, the importance of learning to use digital tools to share your ideas, your vision, and your stories becomes all the more critical.

"Given the choice of drill-and-practice or digital storytelling that is authentic, and involves multiple media forms, which would your students select? I invite you to join the digital storytelling revolution, adding your voice to the mix" (Guhlin, 2009).

"Digital Storytelling" With VoiceThread: Standards Correlations

Students create a storyboard or write a script to accompany their visual images.		
21st-Century Skills	**TESOL Standards**	**TESOL Tech Standards**
• Creativity and Innovation Skills • Critical Thinking and Problem-Solving Skills • Communication and Collaboration Skills • Media Literacy • Productivity and Accountability • Leadership and Responsibility	• Goal 2, Standard 2: Students use English to obtain, process, construct, and provide subject matter information in spoken and written forms. • Goal 2, Standard 3: Students will use appropriate learning strategies to construct and apply academic knowledge.	• Goal 2: Students use technology in socially and culturally appropriate ways. • Goal 3: Students use technology-based tools as aids in the development of their language-learning competence as part of formal instruction and for further learning.

Students record voiceover for a VoiceThread presentation.		
21st-Century Skills	**TESOL Standards**	**TESOL Tech Standards**
• Communication and Collaboration Skills • Social and Cross-Cultural Skills • Information, Media, and Technology Skills • Productivity and Accountability	• Goal 3, Standard 1: Students will use the appropriate language variety, register, and genre according to audience, purpose, and setting. • Goal 3, Standard 2: Students will use nonverbal communication appropriate to audience, purpose, and setting.	• Goal 2: Students use technology in socially and culturally appropriate ways. • Goal 3: Students use technology-based tools as aids in the development of their language-learning competence as part of formal instruction and for further learning.

Students respond to other's visual media through text, audio, or video comments.		
21st-Century Skills	**TESOL Standards**	**TESOL Tech Standards**
• Critical Thinking and Problem-Solving Skills • Information, Media, and Technology Skills • Initiative and Self-Direction • Social and Cross-Cultural Skills	• Goal 1, Standard 1: Students will interact in, through, and with spoken and written English for personal expression and enjoyment.	• Goal 2: Students use technology in socially and culturally appropriate ways.

Guidelines for Using VoiceThread in the Classroom

School librarian Karen Kleigman designed a VoiceThread project called "Federal Holidays: New Holidays Proposals" (available online at http://voicethread.com/#q.b35308.i0.k0). Wes Fryer comments on the best practices he sees in this teacher's project. His comments can serve as guidelines for designing an effective VoiceThread project for your own classroom.

1. **Safety:** Student identities are not revealed. Each student created a custom avatar/icon and used it when sharing their ideas during their project. While I think student photos and first names can be FINE to share with parent permission in VoiceThread projects and other web-published media projects, the approach Karen has taken with this VoiceThread is conservative and safe but still allows the full power of VoiceThread to be utilized and realized. In many conservative communities in the United States where fear about Internet use by young people seems to rival irrational fears about Islamic terrorists lurking behind every corner, publishing without student photos and names is a GREAT way to promote the cause of 21st century literacy development which administrators/school board members can easily understand as well as support.

2. **Multiple Voices:** On each VoiceThread photo page, multiple students who contributed to their project speak and share. Rather than a narrated PowerPoint, this presentation format effectively reveals the different students, personalities, and ideas which contributed to the student project.

3. **Open for Public Commenting:** Karen has left this VoiceThread open for other learners around the world to not only view, but also comment on. This is VITAL. Publishing student work on the "closed web" rather than "the open web" is far less powerful and less beneficial.

Kudos to Karen for modeling best practices and publishing this example of student work on the OPEN WEB, leaving it open for public commenting.

4. **Interaction Welcome:** Published student work in the 21st century should invite ongoing interaction and participation by learners inside and outside the traditional classroom. In 1998 when we published student work in my fourth grade classroom to our school website, it was published in a STATIC form that did not facilitate interaction. The extent of interaction possible at that time was a web project visitor taking the time to send an email to the teacher, whose address was listed at the bottom of the page. Being able to share your voice and ideas interactively in a MODERATED environment (which VoiceThread provides) is critical for the development of 21st century literacy skills. There IS a "big world" out there beyond the walls of the traditional classroom, and inviting others to interact with and provide feedback on the work created by students is an important role for visionary educators and educational leaders in 2008.

Source: Fryer, W. (2008). http://www.speedofcreativity.org/2008/01/23/voicethread-publishing-example-safe-powerful-interactive/

WHEN TO USE VOICETHREAD AND FLICKR WITH ELL'S

VoiceThread and Flickr are used by adults as well as minors. VoiceThread, however, has a section that is meant just for education (http://ed.voicethread.com/). This area is monitored by the Web site itself, and thus is safer for students doing independent work.

Grades K–5

Older elementary students can take digital photos of their school (e.g., the main office, the nurse, the cafeteria, the library, the gym) and create a virtual tour for new students coming in to kindergarten. They can upload the photos to VoiceThread and post spoken or video comments about the events, classes, and celebrations that occur in each place. Kindergarten students can listen and respond with their own questions on the VoiceThread.

Grades 6–8

Middle school students can use Flickr as a multimedia reflective journal by creating a visual interpretation of poetry or young adult literature they are reading in class. They can upload their own digital photos to correspond with the literature or find images already on Flickr to match the mood, setting, plot, and characters of the story, poem, or essay. They can create a "mash up" by using original photos, borrowed images, and text on their Flickr page by pulling the pictures together into one set and commenting on the rationale for choosing each image.

Grades 9–12

High school students can upload images of places in the world that they are studying as a means of creating a visual log of their virtual travels. In the ESL classroom, they can narrate their travels in English in a VoiceThread and ask classmates to comment on their itinerary by posting their own travel suggestions. This project could connect to a social studies class in which the same region could be studied. Music and art could be added by uploading images of artifacts, paintings, and sculptures from museum sites and music clips from the country as well.

As the saying goes, "A picture is worth a thousand words." VoiceThread and Flickr allow students to combine pictures and words in meaningful, original, and exciting ways.

WHO IS USING VOICETHREAD WITH ELL'S?

ESL educator Ronaldo Lima (2008) uses VoiceThread and Flickr with his English language learners to share information about their home countries while practicing speaking and listening skills along with visual literacy. Here, he describes how he designed his first student-generated VoiceThread project.

I HOPE IT WORKS!

The presentation was created by my teenage students using VoiceThread, and it is about the cities they considered to be the 5 most important cities in Brazil. This presentation was published, among other places, in this Student Showcase blog post.

Figure 6.12

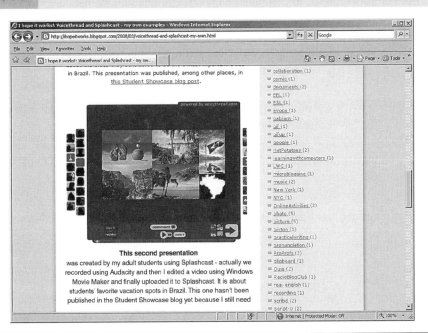

I was inspired by ESL teacher Larry Ferlazzo to join his Sister Classes Project (http://esleflsisterclasses.edublogs.org). I took this chance to spread the word about Brazil and to have my own personal student-generated VoiceThread. What can't be denied is the power that tools such as these have with students.

To prepare the first presentation, I first uploaded the pictures chosen by the students, and, two days later, took them to our school's computer lab for them to record their voices. In the mean time, without advertising the presentation to anyone, we already got our first comment, and it was from a regular VoiceThread user, not an English teacher and not an English student. This gave a unique chance to tell my students that the project they were getting into was extremely meaningful because it would be out there, on the Internet, for actual audience to appreciate, which thrilled them!

As soon as they recorded their voices, I published the presentation in the Students Showcase blog and, after some three weeks, I took them to the computer lab again so that they could answer the questions left to them by project partners' students. In order to get them even more motivated about the project, I asked them to guess how many times they thought their presentation had been viewed so far. Most of them said a number under 100, and only one student was bold enough to guess 120. When I told them that their presentation had been viewed 426 times, they were astonished and, I believe, began to feel the power of publishing on the Internet.

I hope this whole experience will give them a better sense of authorship and readership, for they are producing English (writing in their blogs and speaking in the presentations) for a real audience that is beyond the classroom walls, something difficult to reach in an EFL context. I also hope to help them see that this is the purpose of learning English, after all: to communicate!

Source: Used with permission from Ronaldo Lima. Vignette and screenshot accessed August 16, 2009, at http://ihopeitworks.blogspot.com/2008/03/voicethread-and-splashcast-my-own.html

MAKE YOUR OWN VOICETHREAD

Photo-sharing sites abound on the Internet. If you enjoy taking digital photos, you may already use KodakShare or Snapfish as a means of sharing your images with family and friends. Here are some other sites that lend themselves well to being used in the K–12 educational setting. We have already discussed Flickr and VoiceThread in this chapter. While Picasa is another user-friendly Google product, Photobucket is the number one photo-sharing site in the United States, with over 35 million users. Choose a site that best fits your photo-sharing needs—and those of your students.

Source: Flickr.com

Source: VoiceThread.com

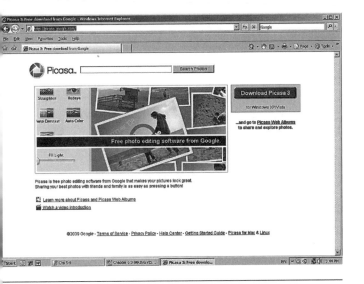

Source: Picasa.Google.com

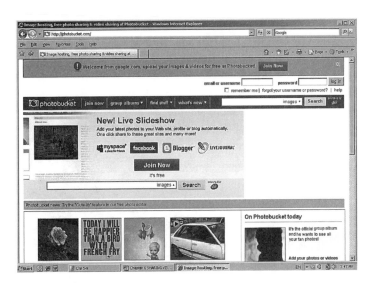

Source: PhotoBucket.com

Creating a VoiceThread can be great fun. But as with other Web 2.0 tools, you first have to open a free account. The great thing about VoiceThread is that the site houses a separate area for educational use only. This ensures that the posts will all be appropriate for K–12 students to view. First go to http://ed.voicethread.com and click on "Sign in or register" on the top right-hand side. This will open up a dialog box that will prompt you for a username and password. If you haven't already registered, click on the word "Register!" below the sign-in boxes.

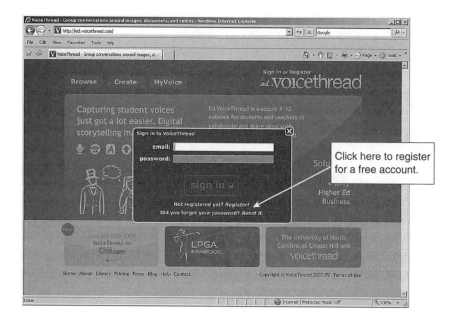

Source: Accessed on May 2, 2009, at http://ed.voicethread.com

You will then be prompted for your name, e-mail address, and a password.

Source: Accessed on May 2, 2009, at http://ed.voicethread.com

Once your account is set up, click on the "create" tab and you will see the available options for uploading photos. It is important that you know where your desired photos reside. For example, are they on your computer in a folder? Are they already uploaded into a photo-sharing site like Flickr? Maybe you already have some interesting photos on your Facebook page? VoiceThread makes it easy to access your photos—even if they are already embedded into another Web 2.0 tool.

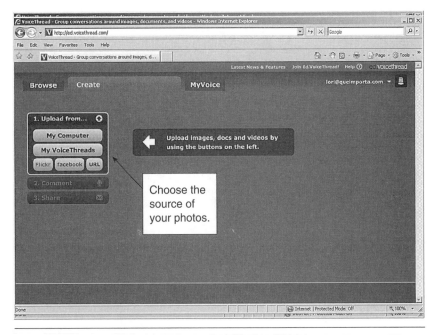

Source: Accessed on May 2, 2009, at http://ed.voicethread.com

As you upload different photos, you can add labels and captions and other information pertinent to each one.

Source: Accessed on May 2, 2009, at http://voicethread.com

Once all your photos are uploaded and labeled, your VoiceThread is ready for comments.

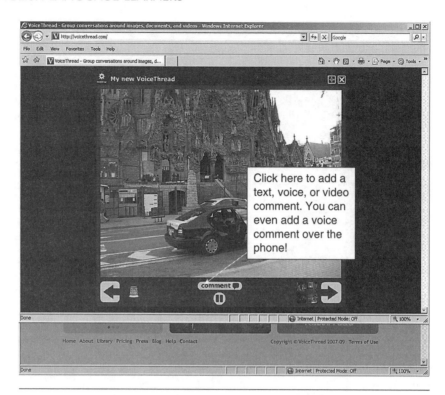

Source: Accessed on May 2, 2009, at http://voicethread.com

Once you are satisfied with your VoiceThread, send the link to friends, colleagues, teachers in other schools, and other classes so that they can comment and share their thoughts about the photos:

Source: Accessed on May 2, 2009, at http://voicethread.com

There are so many uses for VoiceThread—both educational and personal. Find your favorite applications and start sharing your thoughts and images with users from around the world!

WHERE TO FIND MORE INFORMATION ABOUT VOICETHREAD AND FLICKR

REFERENCES

Fryer, W. (2007, July 17). Digital storytelling: Hobby of the present and future. *Ideas and thoughts: Relevant, engaging, authentic learning.* Retrieved August 22, 2009, from http://ideasandthoughts.org/2007/07/16/digital-storytelling-hobby-of-the-present-and-future

Guhlin, M. (2009). *Crafting digital tales and more with Web-based tools.* Retrieved August 22, 2009, from http://mguhlin.wikispaces.com/writings_ds1

SUGGESTED READINGS

The Connected Classroom—digital storytelling with VoiceThread: http://theconnected classroom.wikispaces.com/Digital_Storytelling

Reynolds, G. (2008). *Presentation Zen: Simple ideas on presentation design and delivery.* Berkely, CA: New Riders Press.

Voicethread—a printable guide for teachers: http://voicethread.com/ui/image/classroom.pdf

HELPFUL WEB SITES

Classroom Uses of Flickr—a nice summary on a blog called "The Strength of Weak Ties": http://jakespeak.blogspot.com/2006/03/classroom-uses-of-flickr.html

Getting Started in the Classroom With VoiceThread—this helpful three-page guide offers teachers suggestions for ways to incorporate VoiceThread into the classroom plus information about the options for different educational VoiceThread accounts: http://ed.voicethread.com/media/misc/getting_started_in_the_classroom.pdf

Jakes Online—resources for digital literacy, such as lessons, links, and activities: http://www.jakesonline.org/visual.htm

Language Learning: Using Voicethread for Practicing Speaking Skills—a WikiEducator page with detailed information about setting up an account and designing speaking projects for your students: http://www.wikieducator .org/Using_Voicethread_for_practising_speaking_skills

VoiceThread for EFL and ESL—the official VoiceThread wikipage with activity suggestions and resources: http://voicethread4education.wikispaces.com/EFL+&+ESL

7

Social Networking

Facebook, MySpace, and Twitter

Video connection: Prior to reading this chapter, view the online videos "Social Networking in Plain English" at http://www.commoncraft.com/video-social-networking and "Twitter in Plain English" at http://www.commoncraft.com/twitter

WHAT IS SOCIAL NETWORKING?

Social networking on the World Wide Web involves Web sites or programs that help connect people, establish groups of people with common interests, and facilitate communication and sharing of information.

 NETWORKING

According to Wikipedia, social networking has created new ways to communicate and share information. Social networking websites are being used regularly by millions of people, and it now seems that social networking will be an enduring part of everyday life. The main types of social networking services are those which contain directories of some categories (such as former classmates), means to connect with friends (usually with self-description pages), and recommender systems linked to trust. Popular methods now combine many of these, with MySpace and Facebook being the most widely used in North America. (Wikipedia. Accessed August 17, 2009, at http://en.wikipedia.org/wiki/Social_networking)

Social networking sites provide users with a space for sharing interests and information with other members of their "circle of friends." Once signed up and logged on, users can begin to search for and invite "friends" to have access to their pages and share information. On Facebook, for example, a registered user is given a profile page on which to share information about home contact information, work information, relationship status, birthday, and interests. This information is shared with the friends who have been given permission to access and view your pages.

Along with sharing personal information and photos, social networking sites provide a forum for discussing common interests, fighting for social causes, or sharing music. For example, MySpace is a popular site for up-and-coming bands, many of whom post free mp3 audio files of their music for others to download. Many songs from musical groups and singers have become "cyber-hits" in this way, simply by word of mouth.

Social networking sites can also be created on behalf of celebrities—living and dead. On Facebook you can find pages dedicated to:

- Poets: Jose Marti and Sylvia Plath
- Cartoon characters: Homer Simpson and Spongebob Squarepants
- Actors and actresses: Angelina Jolie and Brad Pitt
- Sports figures: Michael Phelps and Michael Jordan
- Politicians and leaders: George Bush and Barack Obama

These pages have information, images, and links to relevant sites; and, perhaps most importantly, they provide connections to other "fans."

Social networks are also good for sharing hobbies and areas of interest (pages about gardening or chess, for example), information about great restaurants and theater, and even pages for department stores (both Ikea and Target have pages). It is said that in order to be a successful actor, politician, business, or charity, you must have a presence on Facebook.

Twitter is another example of a social network that is seeing more and more popularity among adolescents and adults alike. Twitter is a microblogging platform that allows users to post short updates about their lives. According to the Web site, "Twitter is a service for friends, family, and co-workers to communicate and stay connected through the exchange of quick, frequent answers to one simple question: What are you doing?" (accessed August 17, 2009, at http://twitter.com/). In 140 characters or less, users can type in short "tweets" (as a post to Twitter is called) to broadcast to your followers (anyone who has signed on and been given permission to follow your posts). The service is similar to the "Update Status" feature in Facebook, but differs in that it can be sent via the Internet and via a mobile phone or text messaging service. Twitter represents another way that social networks connect friends and colleagues via a Web-based service.

Components of Social Networking Sites

Social networking sites differ from one site to the next. Elements that seem to remain constant include a profile of the user (including a photo, contact information, likes and dislikes, and a list of groups to which the user belongs) and a list of friends or networks (with links to those friends' pages). Facebook, for example, offers many games and add-ons that make the environment fun and entertaining for users. Some of the most popular applications include a virtual bookshelf (on which you can display images of the covers of books you have read), a list of your favorite movies, CDs, or TV shows, a photo gallery for the sharing of digital images, and a "wall" on which people in your network can write or post messages and pictures.

Figure 7.1

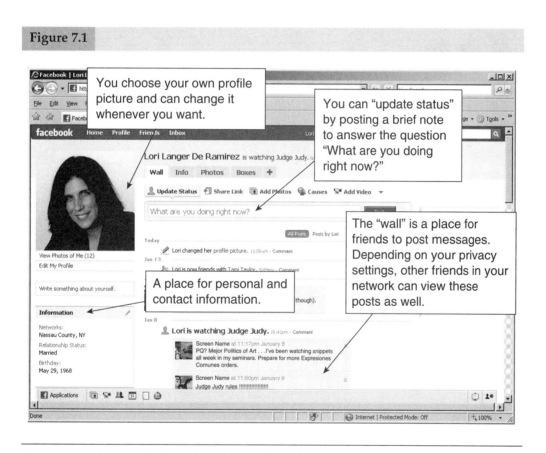

Source: Accessed on May 2, 2009, at http://www.facebook.com/profile.php?success=18id=1215195117

The fun of Facebook is in the sharing of one's "faves" with one's community of friends. Here, we see how a user's friends are listed—using a thumbnail photo of the profile picture plus a name and a link. Depending on the privacy settings, different groups of people can access each other's pages. The second screenshot shows the virtual bookshelf and movie sharing areas of Facebook.

Figure 7.2

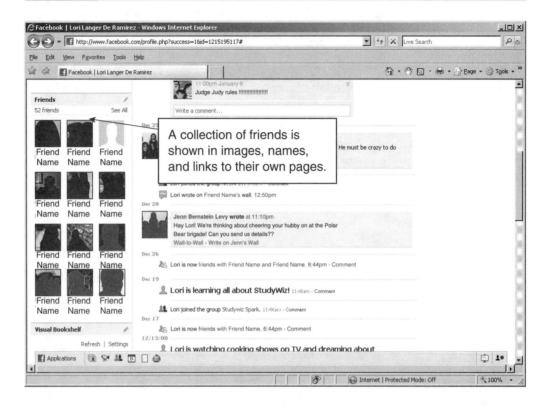

Figure 7.3

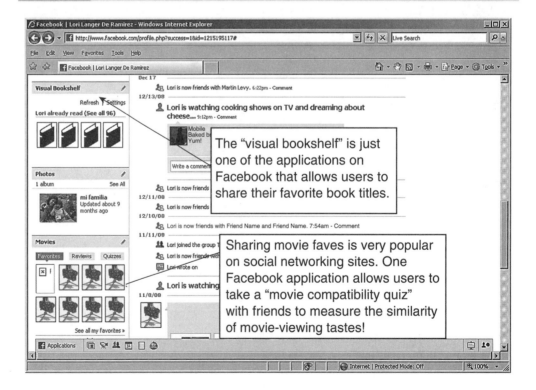

Source: Accessed on May 2, 2009, at http://www.facebook.com/profile.php?success=18id=1215195117#

Communicating on Social Networking Sites

Communication on Facebook and MySpace takes on many forms. Users can send traditional e-mail-like messages through an internal messaging system and an inbox on the profile page. Messages can also be written on the "wall." The most important factor to consider when communicating or posting on any social network is *who will be able to access, and read, your posts or messages.* On all networking sites, users are given choices regarding the permissions that can be set, and thus, who can access your page or receive messages or posts. On Facebook, under the settings drop-down menu, there is an option to set privacy settings. Facebook users can "Control who can see your profile and personal information;" "Control who can search for you, and how you can be contacted;" "Control what stories about you get published to your profile and to your friends' News Feeds;" and "Control what information is available to applications you use on Facebook" (accessed January 14, 2009, at http://www.facebook.com/privacy/?ref=mb). Notice in the screenshot below that this account is set to allow "only friends" to view the information on this user's Facebook pages:

Figure 7.4

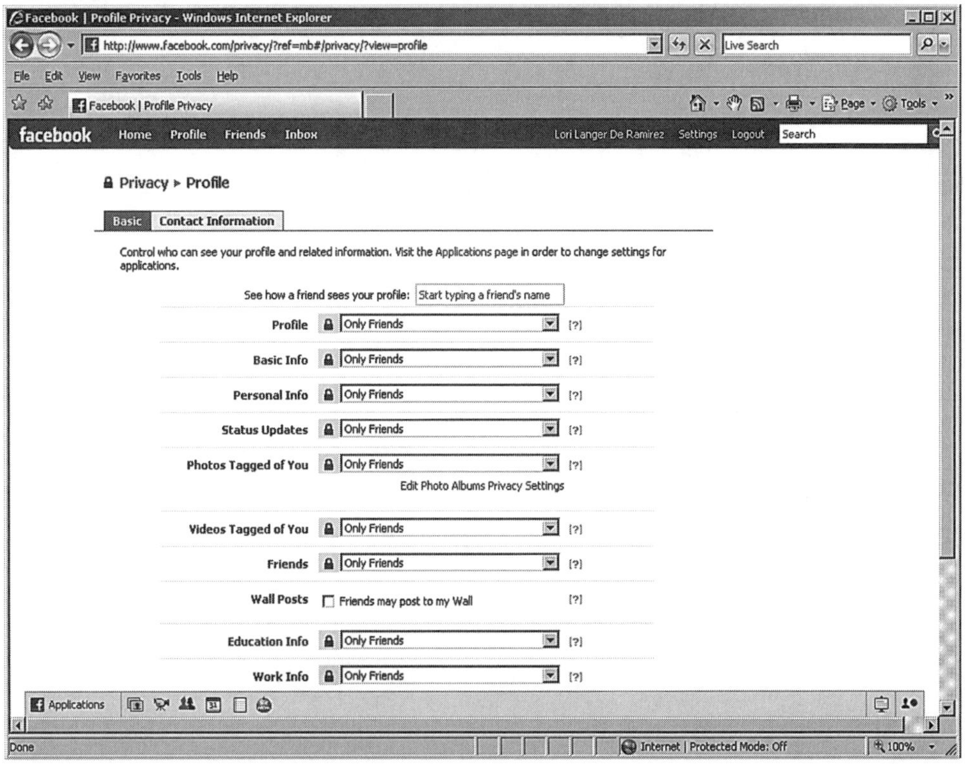

Source: Accessed on May 2, 2009, at http://www.facebook.com/privacy/?ref=mb#/privacy/?view=profile

Social networking sites, like blogs and wikis, can be as open or as closed as a user wishes. For the school setting, it is important that the teacher, parents, administration, and students feel secure in sharing (or not sharing) the information that is on a school-related page or profile. Privacy settings should be used to achieve a comfortable balance between sharing information with the world and feeling safe in cyberspace.

WHY PARTICIPATE IN SOCIAL NETWORKING WITH ELL'S?

Just as Facebook is the most popular social networking site with school-aged students, Twitter seems to be the most popular microblogging system. Here are some of the benefits to using Twitter in an educational setting, as outlined by Gabriela Grosseck and Carmen Holotescu (2008) in this excerpt from their paper "Pedagogical Benefits of Facebook, MySpace and Twitter with ELLs":

Some pragmatic issues (the benefits, the drawbacks, and the logistics) about Twitter as an educational tool, based on literature and some of our own experimentation with it, include the following points:

- *Classroom community.* Twittering in class or outside of it is about learning.
- *Exploring collaborative writing:* It promotes writing as a fun activity, fosters editing skills, and develops literacy skills.
- *Reader response:* Students can use tweets to send out questions and observations to the group while engaged in classroom activities.
- *Collaboration across schools and around the world:* Students can follow tweets from classes studying the same subject or reading the same book in other schools.
- *Project Management:* If you set up a group working on a project, the tweets can be picked up on cell phones (as can e-mail).
- *A tool for assessing opinion, examining consensus, looking for outlying ideas:* Twitter can also be used in an academic setting to foster interaction and debate on a given topic.
- *A viable platform for metacognition* (the practice of thinking about and reflecting on learning), which has been shown to benefit comprehension and retention of information.
- It connects people that one would not have met otherwise.
- It keeps track of a conversation students carry on about a particular topic.
- It's a good way of making a quick announcement.
- Being limited to just 140 characters, Twitter really focuses the attention. Twitter has developed its own sort of discursive grammar set, requiring a great deal of summarizing, which is an important skill to master for ELLs.
- Teachers are connecting their students to the real world.
- It gives the students a sense of what a person is like outside of the classroom (so, they end up being a lot more comfortable with classroom discourse).
- Quieter students, who might not speak up in class, can be heard via tweets.
- It provides age-appropriate environments.

Some other pedagogical applications of Twitter can be dissemination of teachers' publications and materials, locating original sources of ideas and quotes, allowing for very focused and concrete feedback to students to refine their thinking and improve their skills, fostering professional connections, conducting informal research, storytelling, getting feedback on ideas, making appointments, live coverage of events, building trust and building a community.

There are some downsides to Twitter, however, that require some caution:

- The language used on Twitter can be "rude" due to the brevity of each utterance and subsequent occasional lack of courtesy words and phrases.
- The disadvantages for teachers using Twitter is that they are "on call" virtually 24/7 and students can intrude into private time.
- In schools, Twitter also allows much faster spreading of rumors.
- Twitter privacy: In classroom situations, it is better to have a private account.

Source: Used with permission. Adapted Gabriela Grosseck. Paper presented at The 4th International Scientific Conference eLSE "eLearning and Software for Education." Bucharest, April 17–18, 2008. Accessed August 20, 2009, at http://d.scribd.com/docs/2cont12b6rjbmtux8izq.pdf

Facebook and MySpace are both already used in schools as a means of teaching everything from history to health. As an alternative to the traditional research paper, students can be asked to create Facebook pages for famous scientists, historical figures, or an author. They can create a profile and provide background information about their subject. Students play the role of a famous person and imagine what movies he might have liked or what music he might have listened to. For example, were he alive today, Abraham Lincoln might listen to 1960s folk music and enjoy historical fiction. He might read the Harry Potter novels and participate in an animal-rights charity. Depending on the creativity of students, social-networking sites can be a fun way of sharing and organizing information.

Quick List

Use social-networking sites for...

- School club or class pages
- Creating pages for someone famous in your discipline (e.g., a scientist, a sports figure, or a literary character)
- Setting up an events page and inviting people to attend (e.g., have a look at the "Perseids Meteor Shower" on Facebook)
- Fundraising for a service project or charity
- Debating themes in literature, science, history, and so forth
- Sharing videos, music, and other information with students or fellow teachers
- Connecting to other classes around a common topic or theme

HOW TO USE SOCIAL NETWORKING SITES WITH ELL'S: A SAMPLE FACEBOOK LESSON

Not everyone is ready to jump into Facebook during school hours with students. Here is an example of activities that teachers can use *prior* to going online and using a social network—or even in place of an online project. These lesson suggestions involve students in media literacy activities in which they are learning to think critically about social networks and their appropriate uses without actually connecting to Facebook or MySpace.

Warm-Ups

1. **Social Networking:** Walk around the class, and talk to other students about social networking online and offline. Change partners often. After you finish, sit with your original partners and share what you found out.

2. **Chat:** In pairs or groups, decide which of these topics or words from the article "Facebook and MySpace start 'hyper-targeting'" (below) are most interesting and which are most boring.

    Advertising, battles, Web site adverts, personal profiles, private information, Internet users, connecting, messages, Web site pages, online experiences

    Have a chat about the topics you liked.

3. **Private Information:** Are you happy to put your personal information online? With your partners, discuss what kind of personal and financial information on the left you would put on the sites on the right.

Name	Public Forums
Age/Date of birth	Amazon.com
Credit card number	Social networking sites
Address	Online bank
Photo	Your own personal Web site
Marital status	A guest book

4. **Web Opinions:** Which of these opinions do you agree and disagree with? Discuss with your partners.

    - Social networking sites are only for people with poor social skills.
    - One day, we will never need to leave the house: Life will be online.
    - The Internet will be the most dangerous thing in our lives.
    - Someone will steal the identity of a world leader and do bad things with it.
    - People should go back to writing letters. E-mails make us lazy.
    - Social networking will help bring peace to the world.

5. **Advertising:** Spend one minute writing down all of the different words you associate with the word *advertising*. Share your words with your partners, and talk about them.

6. **Quick Debate:** Students A think social networking sites are dangerous. Students B think the opposite. Debate this with your partners. Change partners often.

Have students read or listen to the following article about Facebook and advertising.

Facebook and MySpace Start "Hyper-Targeting"

The world of advertising is set to change as social networking sites open up their pages to advertisers. The sites Facebook and MySpace are now seemingly locked in a battle to win over advertisers by offering them exclusive access to visitors' pages on their websites. Both sites will allow companies to place targeted adverts based on the information their users have provided in their profile. There is a huge amount of data for advertisers to aim at, including geographical details, hobbies, employment, likes and dislikes, and a whole world more. This opens up enormous potential for advertisers for what is now being called 'hyper-targeting.' The sites have calmed fears that private information might be used. MySpace has assured its users that only data they choose to be made public will be available to advertisers.

The social networking sites have hundreds of millions of users, half of whom logon to their personal pages on a daily basis. The sites allow people to connect with others across the globe and are now an important part of people's lives. Facebook CEO Mark Zuckerberg described how his new ads would work: "It's no longer just about messages that are broadcast by companies, but increasingly about information that is shared between friends," he said. Zuckerberg described how advertisers will also use Facebook to advertise: "The core of every user's experience on Facebook is their page and that's where businesses are going to start as well," he explained. He added: "The first thing businesses can do is design a page to craft the exact experience they want people to see." Companies such as Coca Cola, Microsoft and Sony have already signed up.

Source: This lesson was created by Sean Banville from www.BreakingNewsEnglish.com. The accompanying mp3 file is at this site. Accessed August 20, 2009.

Prereading and Listening

1. **True/False:** Look at the article's headline and guess whether these sentences are true (T) or false (F):

    ___ Social networking sites will ban adverts on all of their pages.

    ___ MySpace is in a battle to win advertising space on Facebook's site.

    ___ Social networking site ads will target people's personal information.

    ___ MySpace and Facebook will not target private information.

    ___ About 10% of social networking users logon every day.

    ___ Info that is shared among friends will play a part in the new ads.

    ___ Businesses will also design pages on MySpace and Facebook.

    ___ No multinational company has signed up to advertise on the sites.

After Reading and Listening

1. **Word Search:** Look in your dictionaries/computer to find other meanings, information, and synonyms for the words *social* and *network*.
    - Share your findings with your partners.
    - Make questions using the words you found.
    - Ask your partner or group your questions.

2. **Article Questions:** Look back at the article, and write down some questions you would like to ask the class about the text. Share your questions with other classmates or groups.

3. **Vocabulary:** Circle any words you do not understand. In groups, pool unknown words, and use dictionaries to find their meanings.

4. **Test Each Other:** Look at the words below. With your partner, try to recall exactly how these were used in the text:
   - set
   - locked
   - profile
   - world
   - calmed
   - public
   - whom
   - globe
   - broadcast
   - core
   - craft
   - signed up

Discussion

Student A's Questions (Do not show these to Student B)

a. What did you think when you read the headline?

b. What do you know about MySpace and Facebook?

c. What do you think that, in today's world, new companies can do to become household names overnight?

d. What do you think of social networking?

e. Would you prefer to network online or offline?

f. Do you think there is too much advertising in the world?

g. Would you be happy that companies are targeting your personal information?

h. What do you understand by the term *hyper-targeting*?

i. Do you believe Web sites when they say they will keep your personal information safe?

Student B's Questions (Do not show these to Student A)

a. Did you like reading this article?

b. Do you think most of the world will be online social networkers one day?

c. What do you think of the speed with which we can now communicate with each other across the globe?

d. Is the Internet an important part of your life?

e. Would you want the information you share between your friends to be used to target adverts?

f. Facebook says the targeted ads will be exactly those that users might want to see. What do you think of this?

g. Are you interested in seeing how this new advertising system will work?

h. What questions would you like to ask Mark Zuckerberg?

i. Did you like this discussion?

Homework

1. **Vocabulary Extension:** Choose several of the words from the text. Use a dictionary or Google's search field (or another search engine) to build up more associations and collocations of each word.

2. **Internet:** Search the Internet and find more information about MySpace and Facebook. Talk about what you discover with your partners in the next lesson.

3. **Social Networking:** Make a poster about Internet sites that require you to upload personal information. Compare and contrast the dangers and benefits of sharing personal information online. Show your poster to your classmates in the next lesson. Did you all include similar things?

4. **Magazine Article:** Write a magazine article about social networking and its benefits and dangers. Include imaginary interviews with parents and site CEOs. Read what you wrote to your classmates in the next lesson. Write down new words and expressions.

5. **Letter:** Write a letter to Mark Zuckerberg, the CEO of Facebook. Ask him three questions about his site. Give him three pieces of advice on how to make it better. Read your letter to your partners in your next lesson. Your partners will answer your questions.

It is not always possible—or preferable—to go online with students in school to explore a particular Web 2.0 tool. With social networks becoming *de rigeur* in the lives of young people, it is important not just to know how to use these technologies but also how to be critical of them and use them safely and wisely. This series of activities helps students to see the broader ramifications of social networking without being too pedantic or preachy. Students are given the opportunity to take a step back and discuss critically their particular relationships with sites like Facebook and MySpace with classmates, who are involved in the same practices. The activities also focus ELLs on particular language structures and vocabulary that strengthen speaking, listening, reading, and writing skills. In the following chart, we can see how these activities connect to the different national standards for TESOL and 21st-Century Skills.

Sample Facebook Lesson: Standards Correlations

Students read or listen to a news report about new Facebook advertising policies.		
21st-Century Skills	**TESOL Standards**	**TESOL Tech Standards**
• Core Subjects and 21st-Century Themes • Media Literacy • Information Literacy	• Goal 2, Standard 2: Students use English to obtain, process, construct, and provide subject-matter information in spoken and written forms. • Goal 2, Standard 3: Students will use appropriate learning strategies to construct and apply academic knowledge.	• n/a

Students discuss and question the importance of Facebook and other social networking sites in their lives.		
21st-Century Skills	**TESOL Standards**	**TESOL Tech Standards**
• Critical Thinking and Problem-Solving Skills • Communication and Collaboration Skills • Media Literacy • Information Literacy	• Goal 2, Standard 1: Students will use English to interact in the classroom. • Goal 2, Standard 2: Students use English to obtain, process, construct, and provide subject-matter information in spoken and written forms. • Goal 3, Standard 1: Students will use the appropriate language variety, register, and genre according to audience, purpose, and setting.	• Goal 3: Students use technology-based tools as aids in the development of their language-learning competence as part of formal instruction and for further learning.

Students search for and define new vocabulary words and structures through reading and writing about the topic of social networking.

21st-Century Skills	TESOL Standards	TESOL Tech Standards
• Critical Thinking and Problem-Solving Skills • Core Subjects and 21st-Century Themes	• Goal 2, Standard 2: Students use English to obtain, process, construct, and provide subject-matter information in spoken and written forms. • Goal 2, Standard 3: Students will use appropriate learning strategies to construct and apply academic knowledge.	• Goal 3: Students use technology-based tools as aids in the development of their language-learning competence as part of formal instruction and for further learning.

Rules for Social Networking Online

When posting on a microblogging site like Twitter, it is helpful to think about the parameters of your project and posts. Here are some good rules to follow.

For Twitter to work best in an educational setting, one should adopt certain measures, as follows:

- Before using Twitter in the classroom, share with students some of the abbreviations and the lingo of Twitter.

- In discussions with the class, come to some consensus about what topics to include—and to avoid—in your tweets.

- Don't be afraid of retweeting a request so that people who have just logged in can pick it up.

- Be flexible and prepared for the direction that the tweets can take you.

- Be open to reflecting on what aspects of Twitter worked and didn't work with your classes.

- Consider implementing this approach on a pilot or trial basis with a selected group of students or a selected class.

- There should be a mix of the old and the new (it should be possible for students to achieve the intended learning objectives of the lesson by alternative routes, especially for students who don't have access to the Internet or computers at home).

- Students should be included in the evaluation of the activity.

- Allow your network time to respond. (Some times of the day are busier than others. The number of people online in your school at a particular time will affect the speed of the messaging system.)

- Twitter is meaningless without a network, which should be willing to share, engage, provoke, and discuss topics of relevance to the whole group.

Source: Adapted from Grosseck, G. and Holotescu, C. Used with permission from Gabriela Grosseck. Paper presented at The 4th International Scientific Conference eLSE "eLearning and Software for Education." Bucharest, April 17–18, 2008. Accessed August 20, 2009, at http://d.scribd.com/docs/2cont12b6rjbmtux8izq.pdf

WHEN TO USE SOCIAL NETWORKING WITH ELL'S

Media literacy is especially important for students using social networking sites. It is crucial that young people understand the privacy settings on these sites and be able to make informed judgments about appropriate material to post on their pages. To this end, some activities surrounding acceptable uses of social networks would be beneficial to all grade levels. There are also many activities that can incorporate the direct use of different social networking sites into the K–12 ESL classroom.

Grades K–5

Have students think about a character in a book you have read as a class. Brainstorm what a Facebook profile might look like for this character. What picture would he use for his page? Who would the character's friends be? For example, if Dora the Explorer had a page (she already does, by the way!), who would be her friends? What would be her hobbies? Based on the story read in class, design a page as a class that reflects the character's personality. For older or more advanced students, each student can choose her own character and create a page.

On Twitter, elementary students might connect with classrooms in a different country to compare and contrast the typical school day in both places. The teachers could send tweets out to the other school indicating change in classes, a new topic being studied, time for recess, and other classroom activities. After a period of time exchanging daily tweets, students could then compare and contrast a typical school day in the two schools.

Grades 6–8

Adolescent students can visit "cause" pages to learn about a variety of charities and nonprofit organizations that have pages on Facebook. They can learn about the charity from the information on the page and from posts from supporters and visitors. Based on the information, they can design a service project to help the organization and then post their results to the page. Alternately, students can design their own page for a fundraising event for the benefit of a local charity or nonprofit organization in the community.

Grades 9–12

More mature students can use Facebook as a means of running school clubs or sharing information about particular classes. They can also open a page to facilitate a debate on a particular topic, inviting classmates to join as friends in order to post comments on the wall in support of their side of the debate. Note that this is already a use of Facebook that will be familiar to students. Many pages already exist in support of political views, social issues, and current-events topics. Sometimes, the discussions on these pages can get heated, so teachers should monitor a school-sponsored debate page as much as possible.

Livemocha.com is a free Web site created just for the purpose of practicing foreign languages. Students who study a language in school set up an account on the site and connect with native speakers of the language they are studying. They can learn and practice the language and then share and connect with others.

Figure 7.5

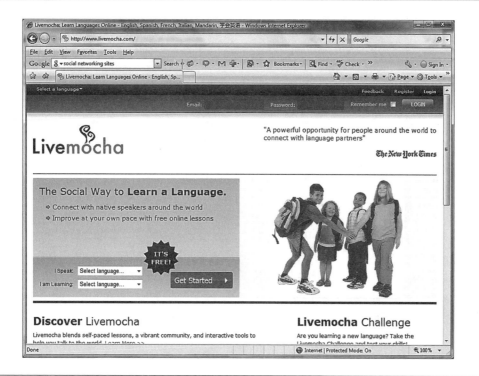

Source: Accessed on May 14, 2009, at http://www.livemocha.com

WHO IS USING SOCIAL NETWORKING WITH ELL'S?

Steve McCrea teaches in a language school in Fort Lauderdale, Florida. His articles on technology and ESOL instruction are available by contacting him at freeenglishlessons@gmail.com. Let's read his tips and suggestions for using Facebook in the classroom based on his own experiences with his ESL classes. In this narrative, Steve shares some benefits of—and also some warnings about—using social networking sites with students in schools.

USING FACEBOOK IN THE ESOL CLASSROOM

Social networking is a hot topic for many students. Five years ago, email was the top way for students to keep in touch with each other. Up to a year ago, Skype and MSN messenger (or AIM, America Online's version) were the popular ways to network. Now Orkut, MySpace and Facebook lead the way. Facebook is regularly in the top five of the world's most-accessed web sites.

I teach students from Asia, Europe and South America (ages 15 to 45), and I try to keep in touch with students after class and after they leave our school. Many of the newcomers want to keep in touch with the teacher on weekends for a variety of reasons:

1. *Some students want some tips on "what to see and do" in our area.*

2. *Diligent students want extra feedback on their writing, so I urge them to write to me. I can mark their essays while I watch TV (and my typing is easier to read than my handwriting).*

I noticed about a year ago that many students in my ESL classes were using social networking sites fairly consistently. To further investigate, I opened an account on Facebook and developed the following observations and tips for my colleagues about the benefits of social networking sites in the classroom.

1. *Facebook is easier than email. Students find Facebook an engaging way to interact, so why not take advantage of it? I might have six students named "Jin," but each has a different profile photo—so it's easier than email to identify a way to contact them. It's not an effort for most students to look at my messages.*

2. *Facebook can encourage the practice of writing. The short messages that I write to my students stimulate them to write in reply.*

3. *Facebook is more reliable than email. Students might check their email three times a week. They'll check their Facebook page three or four times a day.*

4. *Facebook gets through (and my email might be called spam). When I send a bulk message by email to fifteen students, my message can be treated as junk mail by many programs. Facebook allows me to send my message quickly to groups of my students.*

5. *Facebook encourages interactions. When new students join a class, I can quickly get them integrated with the rest of our class by linking new students with their classmates on Facebook. By becoming Facebook "friends," the real-life friendships actually grow more quickly.*

6. *Facebook can be used for language practice. If the student switches the Web site's language to English, then the user can practice reading English. If they are still struggling with the language and need some bilingual support, they can switch their settings to their home language (Facebook currently supports over 35 languages on their site).*

7. *Facebook's "applications" are more than games. Applications are ways to enhance skills of presentation and persuasion. I ask each student to create a "fan group" (facebook.com/groups/create.php) for their favorite applications or for their favorite musicians. I ask them to find a fun application (e.g., Knighthood, Yagura, Green Patch, and Blue Cove) and then teach us how to use it.*

8. *Facebook has competition. Since there are other forms of social networking, the students in my classes have an opportunity to compare the different versions. While my Brazilian students prefer Orkut.com, Thai students like hi5.com and Koreans use cyworld.com. In a mixed classroom, students can make presentations about their favorite networking sites and then compare the pros and cons of each.*

There are some challenges, however, to using Facebook. Here are some of the downsides to consider:

1. *The games look like games! Without guidance and structure, the use of these applications can quickly turn into a party. It helps to have a list of target vocabulary and a list of steps and goals for each activity where a student uses an application.*

2. *Many applications are repetitive and annoying. The idea behind many applications on Facebook is to encourage interactions: give a "virtual present" and receive one, or invite more friends to participate in the activity. The repeated requests for participation disturbs many "friends" and encourages discussion groups to collect "friends" only for racing virtual cars (Eco Racer) or keeping fish (in an activity called "Blue Cove"). These applications may distract from language learning.*

3. *Facebook can be addictive. Look out: Once students know that you like Facebook, you might find dozens of messages. However, you might also find it easier to keep in touch with students through Facebook than through email and more fun—and even more efficient—to assign homework via Facebook.*

4. *Some students don't want to get on Facebook. My Brazilian students prefer Orkut.com, so I used to end up doubling the time I spent uploading photos and videos to my accounts. To avoid this, I reserve time in the media lab of our school and pair European and Brazilian students. The Brazilians show the Europeans some language learning movies that I posted on my Orkut account, and then students with Facebook show movies that I posted on my Facebook account.*

5. *Facebook's movies must be shorter than two minutes. At first, this limitation appeared to be a liability (since many of my teaching "video moments" on youtube.com are between three and five minutes). But it turned out to be a benefit, since many of my students have a short attention span (especially after lunch!)*

Here's an example of a handout that I use when I want to introduce new vocabulary through a Facebook activity called Yagura.

Hello, Student. This activity begins in your FACEBOOK account. If you don't have a Facebook account, you can register or you can work with a student who has a Facebook account.

1. *Click on Friends tab*

2. *Scroll down to Find People*

3. *Type your teacher's email address (connected to a Facebook account) and click Search*

4. *Click on Add as Friend*

5. *Then tell the teacher that your invitation has been sent. (The teacher needs to accept you as a friend.)*

6. *Next, look for the reply from the teacher. You will receive an invitation to join Yagura. You will need to accept the activity ("allow access"). [Note: If you are impatient, you can search for Yagura in the Search box on your Facebook account. Select the first Yagura in the list and activate the activity.]*

7. *Read the instructions ("How to Play")*

8. *Click on the first game (how to cook tempura shrimp)*

Vocabulary practice (do you know all of these words?)

flour	cube	wok
prawn tempura	scramble	pan
slice	boil	a hot pad
dice	broil	a trivet
grill	roast	a spatula
grind	pour	a blender
mash	sprinkle	a ladle
smash	blend	
chop	pot	

When you are finished with the first game, send "virtual food" to your Facebook friends, including the teacher.

If you still have time before the end of the class, you can try a second activity (preparing noodle soup).

Source: McCrea, S. (2008, December 28). Accessed August 26, 2009, at http://www.freeeng lishlessons.com/articlelive/articles/5/1/More-About-Using-Facebook-in-the-ESOL-Classroom/ Page1.html

JOIN A SOCIAL NETWORKING SITE

Joining a social networking site is as easy as filling out a form or a survey. As with blogs and wikis, you open a free account by providing an e-mail or ID and a password. In the United States, the most popular social networks are Facebook and MySpace. Twitter is the most popular microblogging site. Ning is a metasite that allows users to create their own social networks and Web sites.

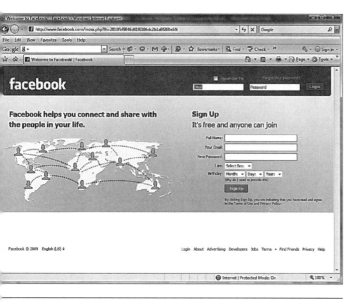

Source: Facebook.com

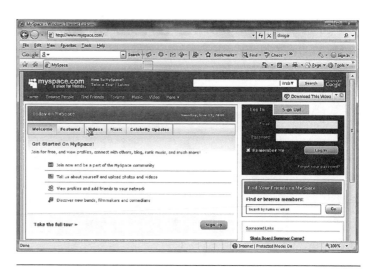

Source: MySpace.com

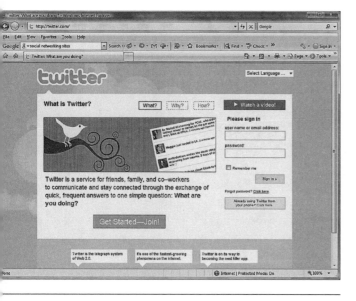

Source: Twitter.com

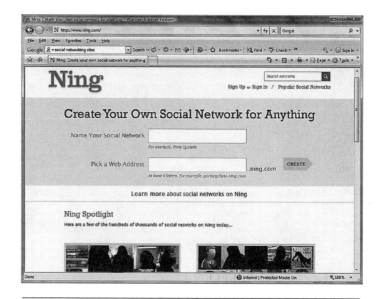

Source: Ning.com

Most people choose a social networking site for personal use based on its popularity with their friends. For educational use, choices are made based on ease of use, student popularity, and security settings.

Once you choose a site that appeals to you and your students, sign up for a free account by choosing a username (or providing an e-mail address) and a password. Most of the sites have a clearly marked "sign up here" link on their homepage. By clicking on this link, you will be taken to pages that ask for more information. Some of the information is required (normally a valid e-mail address, first and last name, and date of birth) and some information is optional (marital status, address, religion). As long as the required information is provided, you do not have to add the optional information.

Source: Accessed on May 14, 2009, at http://signups.myspace.com/index.cfm?fuseaction=signupy

After you set up an account, you can customize your page by rearranging blocks of information and by adding applications of your choice.

Source: Accessed on May 2, 2009, at http://www.facebook.com/home.php#/profile.php?id=1215195117&v=box_3&viewas=1215195117

Social networking can be an efficient way of connecting with your students and an exciting way of sharing information with groups—and even with classrooms from around the world. Students already enjoy social networking and will be excited by the idea of bringing their online world into the ESL classroom.

● ● ●

WHERE TO FIND MORE INFORMATION ABOUT SOCIAL NETWORKING

SUGGESTED READINGS

Andrews, R. (2007, April 19). Don't tell your parents: Schools embrace MySpace. *Wired Magazine*. Retrieved August 20, 2009, from http://www.wired.com/culture/education/news/2007/04/myspaceforschool

Gross, D. B. (2009). *Tools for teaching*. Jossey-Bass.

Magid, L., & Collier, A. (2006). *MySpace unraveled: A parent's guide to teen social networking*. Peachpit Press.

Mason, R. (2008). *E-learning and social networking handbook: Resources for higher education*. Routledge.

Thelwall, M. (2008, January 25). MySpace, Facebook, Bebo: Social networking students. *Association for Learning Technology Online Newsletter*. Retrieved August 20, 2009, from http://newsletter.alt.ac.uk/e_article000993849.cfm?x=b11,0,w

HELPFUL WEB SITES

Education Applications on Facebook—a directory of applications that currently exist on Facebook with an educational purpose or educational content: http://www.facebook.com/apps/index.php?q=education

Educators Using Facebook—a social network of teachers who use social networks! Teachers post questions, share problems, success stories and lesson ideas: http://www.classroom20.com/group/educatorsusingfacebook

How to Protect Your Privacy on Facebook—watch a short video that shows you how to set the privacy settings on Facebook: http://sitening.com/blog/how-to-protect-your-privacy-on-facebook-screencast

Pros and Cons of MySpace and Facebook—a detailed discussion plus links about the strengths and challenges to using social networking sites in the classroom: http://www.helium.com/items/527905-pros-and-cons-of-myspace-and-facebook

The Facebook Classroom: 25 Facebook Apps That Are Perfect for Online Education—this site was developed with college students in mind, but many of the applications work well with middle and high school students: http://www.collegedegree.com/library/college-life/15-facebook-apps-perfect-for-online-education

Social Bookmarking

Diigo and Del.icio.us

Video connection: Prior to reading this chapter, view the online video "Social Bookmarking in Plain English" at http://www.commoncraft.com/bookmarking-plain-english

WHAT IS SOCIAL BOOKMARKING?

Social bookmarking involves the creation of a list of your favorite sites housed not on your laptop or PC but rather in cyberspace. It is a virtual collection of your favorite places to visit on the World Wide Web. Social bookmarking sites like Diigo.com and Del.icio.us.com provide users with space on the Web on which to collect, file, and share bookmarks and favorite sites.

 DIIGO

Diigo (which is an acronym that stands for Digest of Internet Information, Groups and Other stuff) not only allows users to bookmark sites but also to add highlights and annotations. According to the Web site,

> Diigo provides a browser add-on that can really improve your research productivity. As you read on the web, instead of just bookmarking, you can highlight portions of web pages that are of particular interest to you. You can also attach sticky notes to specific parts of web pages. Unlike most other web "highlighters" that merely clip, Diigo highlights and sticky notes are persistent in the sense that whenever you return to the original web page, you will see your highlights and sticky notes superimposed on the original page, just what you would expect if you highlighted or wrote on a book!

Source: Accessed August 21, 2009, at http://www.diigo.com/about

Surely, you have had this experience: You bookmark some wonderful site at home only to find that at school you can't find the site again. You may have also wanted to take notes or highlight some content, but you just can't highlight a computer screen!

Diigo and Del.icio.us give you a way to bookmark sites online—and the resulting list of bookmarks can be accessed from any computer with an Internet connection. Diigo gives users the extra advantage of being able to annotate—and thus make personal—favorite Web pages. Users can highlight important words or phrases or add a virtual sticky note with the user's comments relating to the page. While this might sound like simply an improvement on traditional bookmarking, there is much more to social bookmarking than simply collecting sites on the Web. Social bookmarking—as the name portends—is yet another way of creating a professional or educational network with others who share similar interests. By making your bookmarks and annotations public, colleagues, students, and others can access your links and even add them to their own collection. In the school setting, students are often asked to visit specific Web sites in order to answer some questions or retrieve certain information. The teacher might want to limit the Web sites that the student visits and could create a Diigo or Del.icio.us list that they would access, making use of those links only. Or, a group could be created on Diigo with all the students' links being pooled into it. Here is an example of a group for ESL teachers and students called "ESL Tools":

Figure 8.1

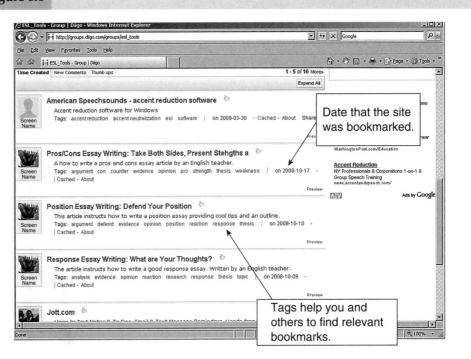

Source: Accessed on August 21, 2009, at http://groups.diigo.com/groups/esl_tools

Components of Social Bookmarking Sites

By logging in to a personal Diigo account, users access recent saves, the most popular Web sites, and the latest headlines.

Figure 8.2

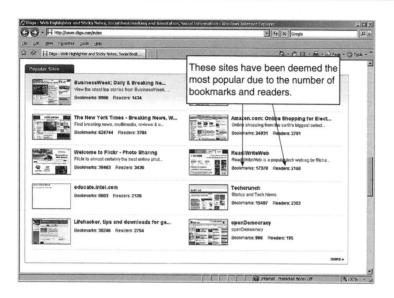

Source: Accessed August 21, 2009, at http://www.diigo.com/index

Diigo also serves as an RSS feed reader (refer to the Chapter 4, on podcasts, for more information about subscriptions and RSS feeds). Users can manage subscriptions and organize them using key terms and phrases to facilitate research and sharing.

Figure 8.3

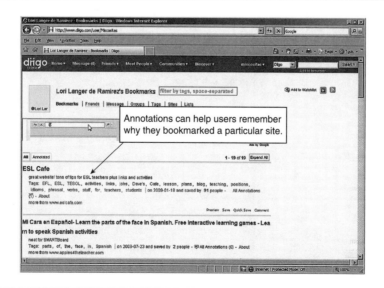

Source: Accessed May 2, 2009, at http://www.diigo.com/user/Miscositas

WHY PARTICIPATE IN SOCIAL BOOKMARKING WITH ELL'S?

The uses of social bookmarking Web sites range from the personal to the academic. Diigo offers a rationale for using its services in the classroom:

> Diigo enables effective collaborative research. You can easily share your findings, complete with your highlights and sticky notes, with friends and colleagues. A project team, a class, or a club can create a group on Diigo to pool relevant resources, findings and thoughts together.

Source: Accessed August 21, 2009, at http://www.diigo.com/about

By sharing and annotating Web sites that you have found valuable, friends and colleagues can gain knowledge, save time, and get some insight into your interests and hobbies. In schools, social bookmarking is an excellent means of facilitating research, doing group assignments, and sharing important links with students. Since sites like Diigo allow users to annotate links, group them, and share them with others, social bookmarking is a useful tool for collaborative work online.

Social bookmarking sites also reflect the idea that there is wisdom in numbers. When Web sites are bookmarked, many social bookmarking services will show users how many other members have also bookmarked the site. When hundreds or thousands of members have chosen the same site, it is likely that it is a particularly useful or popular site—and thus worth looking at or adding to your own list of bookmarks. For this reason, a social bookmarking tool can facilitate the discussion of media literacy topics such as the validity and authenticity of Web sites and sources. For ELLs—and all students—it is crucial to be able to determine which sites are valid and reliable and which ones are not. Social bookmarking helps by sharing information about the person or people who tagged a site and also a rationale for why the site has been chosen.

Diigo and Del.icio.us connect users by common interest or research topics. Students can link to others doing similar work in different schools or even other countries. These connections can serve as the basis for collaborative projects between classrooms. For these reasons, social bookmarking sites can also be a form of social networking in which students in different regions of the world can cocreate knowledge and find information together in cyberspace.

Quick List

Use social bookmarking sites for . . .

- Team research projects
- Webquests
- Taking notes directly on a Web page
- Annotating text
- Asking questions regarding confusing information
- Collecting research data
- Collaborating on group projects
- Finding new information via social networks

HOW TO USE SOCIAL BOOKMARKING WITH ELL'S: THE BEST SOCIAL BOOKMARKING APPLICATIONS

Larry Ferlazzo is a well-known ESL educator and a passionate blogger (visit his excellent blog: "Larry Ferlazzo's Websites of the Day for Teaching ELL, ESL & EFL" at http://larryferlazzo.edublogs.org/). In one of his blog posts, he explores the many social bookmarking sites and comments on the ways that each might be used with English language learners:

> Social bookmarking means being able to easily save the addresses of specific sites you're looking at and want to revisit, and then being able to share those with others. Even though I don't use a social bookmarking site a lot (since I post most sites I find on my blog), when I do use one I use del.icio.us. Below is a list of my picks for some of the other excellent social bookmarking applications along with some ways in which they can be used with English Language Learners:
>
> **Blerp** (www.Blerp.com) Once you register (which is extraordinarily easy and doesn't require activation by email), you type in a webpage address, click on "post" and you can type on a virtual post-it note and place it anywhere on the text of the page and you are then given the page's URL with the notes. It's extremely user-friendly. It also allows you to see what other readers of the same page have written. All those virtual post-it notes are listed on the side of the page. All you have to do is click on a note and it magically appears at the location on the page where it was placed. I believe a lot of the things many web tools allow you to do are neat, but don't necessarily provide much "value-added" benefit to doing the same task using non-tech tools. Even the other tools on the "website annotating" best list only let you do the exact same thing you can do with hard copy. With Blerp, however, after students have completed demonstrating their reading strategies, they can then see what everybody else has written, too.
>
> **2Collab** (www.2Collab.com) is a collaborative bookmarking application. You can create your own group with various privacy options, share bookmarks (including visual snapshots of webpages), and leave comments about the ones you submit and the ones others in the group contribute. The privacy and group options, along with the commenting feature, really make this site stand out for educational purposes.
>
> **Web2Wave** (www.Web2Wave.com) is a visual bookmarking site in 3D that I think has a lot of educational potential for both English Language Learners and mainstream students. It allows you to create "tabs" where you can categorize visual images of websites you'd like to bookmark. You can write a short description

for each website and categorize them in each "tab." Then, you can view your bookmarked sites in a pretty cool 3D carousel. It appears to show the page you want to bookmark almost immediately and also allows you to bookmark images, which would provide even more opportunities for categorization exercises.

oSkope (oSkope.com) is an excellent bookmarking site for images. Users first search the Web for images. Then you can drag-and-drop the ones you want into a "My Folder." Next, you can write about them as a group and email the My Folder link to yourself or a teacher to be posted on an online journal or blog. It couldn't be easier. However, right now you don't have the ability to write a tag or description under each photo you put in My Folder, but they're planning on adding that in the very near future.

Tizmos (http://www.Tizmos.com) is a super-easy way for users to save thumbnail images (and links) of their favorite websites on one page. Twice a week I bring my Intermediate English class to the computer lab, and it would be an easy way for each student to identify their favorites from among the 8,000 links on my website. In addition, I can place a link to each student's Tizmos page on my website so that the whole class can see each other's choices. The advantage Tizmos has over the sites listed here is that it's just so darn easy to set-up and use!

Sqworl (sqworl.com) is an easy way for English Language Learner students to bookmark thumbnail images (and their related links) of sites they're interested in. It's especially easy to create separate "groups" of sites with tags, which could be handy for research and other tasks. Since it also lets you grab images off the web, it's possible for students to create categories, for example, of images around a unit of study and write descriptions.

Viewista (www.viewista.com/) is similar to the last two tools. One neat feature of Viewista is that it allows various options on how to view the multiple sites, including vertically and through a slideshow mode.

StHrt (sthrt.com/) is a web application for creating personal home pages and, in many ways, is similar to both Sqworl and Tizmos. Those two tools are tools my students use for easily saving favorite links (i.e., for research they're doing) as thumbnail images and sharing them with others. The visual thumbnails and ease of use make all three of these applications particularly accessible to English Language Learners.

Source: Used with permission from Larry Ferlazzo, author. Accessed August 21, 2009, at http://larryferlazzo.edublogs.org/2008/04/16/the-best-social-bookmarking-applications-for-english-language-learners-other-students

The Best Social Bookmarking Applications: Standards Correlations

Students research, collect, and bookmark pertinent reference materials (Web sites) online.		
21st-Century Skills	**TESOL Standards**	**TESOL Tech Standards**
• Core Subjects and 21st-Century Themes • Critical Thinking and Problem-Solving Skills • Media Literacy • Information Literacy • Initiative and Self-Direction	• Goal 2, Standard 1: To use English to achieve academically in all content areas: Students will use English to obtain, process, construct, and provide subject-matter information in spoken and written forms. • Goal 2, Standard 3: Students will use appropriate learning strategies to construct and apply academic knowledge.	• Goal 1: Language learners demonstrate foundational knowledge and skills in technology for a multilingual world. • Goal 3: Language learners effectively use and critically evaluate technology-based tools as aids in the development of their language-learning competence as part of formal instruction and for further learning.

Students annotate and organize bookmarks with their own comments and information.		
21st-Century Skills	**TESOL Standards**	**TESOL Tech Standards**
• Core Subjects and 21st-Century Themes • Media Literacy • Information Literacy • Initiative and Self-Direction • Flexibility and Adaptability	• Goal 2, Standard 2: To use English to achieve academically in all content areas: Students will use English to obtain, process, construct, and provide subject-matter information in spoken and written form. • Goal 2, Standard 3: To use English to achieve academically in all content areas: Students will use appropriate learning strategies to construct and apply academic knowledge.	• Goal 1: Language learners demonstrate foundational knowledge and skills in technology for a multilingual world. • Goal 2: Language learners use technology in socially and culturally appropriate, legal, and ethical ways.

Students share their bookmarks and comment on each other's links.		
21st-Century Skills	**TESOL Standards**	**TESOL Tech Standards**
• Core Subjects and 21st-Century Themes • Media Literacy • Information Literacy • Initiative and Self-Direction • Flexibility and Adaptability • Social and Cross-Cultural Skills • Communication and Collaboration Skills	• Goal 2, Standard 2: To use English to achieve academically in all content areas: Students will use English to obtain, process, construct, and provide subject-matter information in spoken and written forms. • Goal 2, Standard 3: To use English to achieve academically in all content areas: Students will use appropriate learning strategies to construct and apply academic knowledge. • Goal 3, Standard 1: To use English in socially and culturally appropriate ways: Students will use the appropriate language variety, register, and genre according to audience, purpose, and setting.	• Goal 1: Language learners demonstrate foundational knowledge and skills in technology for a multilingual world. • Goal 2: Language learners use technology in socially and culturally appropriate, legal, and ethical ways.

Social Bookmarking Etiquette

Here are some tips and rules of thumb for being a responsible and courteous social bookmarker:

- **Submit Quality Contents:** Content is the bread and butter, the heart and soul of all social bookmarking sites. People visit popular bookmarking sites for their content. Submitting quality articles, photos, and videos will help the bookmarking sites' growth.
- **Be Courteous:** Remember that social bookmarking sites form a community. There are different demographics in different sites. As

a citizen of whichever bookmarking site, please be courteous towards other bookmarkers—especially to new ones. You are representing a community, you don't want your community to be reputed as rude, hostile, or vulgar.

- **Be a Responsible Bookmarker:** Keep your profile clean by having a decent avatar, articles tagged well, and putting everything in the right categories or groups' niches. These help bookmarking sites to look cleaner and have better navigation.
- **Quality Over Quantity:** Bookmarking sites should deliver quality contents to the readers; thus, poor quality contents can clutter around the bookmarking sites, which can cost [the site] its credibility.
- **Interact:** Social bookmarking is not all about submissions and bookmarking. It's also about participating and interacting with other bookmarkers. One way we can help bookmarking sites to deliver quality contents efficiently is by voting and commenting.

Source: Used with permission from Jed Chan. Accessed August 21, 2009, at http://jedchan.com/contribute-success-social-bookmarking-sites

WHEN TO USE SOCIAL BOOKMARKING WITH ELL'S

Social bookmarking sites have applications for students across the K–12 continuum. Any time a class or student creates a traditional bookmark for a preferred Web site, they might be encouraged to use social bookmarking tools, thus creating a collection of sites that can be annotated, edited, and shared with peers and classmates.

Grades K–5

Diigo and Del.icio.us and other social bookmarking sites can be used with elementary aged students to collect class Web sites and to share them with caregivers at home. Teachers can find appropriate and useful Web sites and collect them on a Diigo page, for example, for students to access and use for research, homework, and group projects. They can create a class group to house and organize the bookmarks that the class finds useful throughout the year.

Grades 6–8

Adolescents can use social bookmarking sites as a means of doing group research projects or keeping track of their favorite sites for language practice. They can develop groups that help in doing team projects and other collaborative work across the curriculum. They can be asked to comment on and critique each other's collections of links as a means of strengthening media literacy skills.

Grades 9–12

To use social bookmarking sites on the secondary level, students can create lists of excellent research-related Web sites and rate the sites for their classmates. They can write reviews and summaries of the best Web sites and add them to a class page for other students to share. Students can also post "sticky notes" to sites with questions or summaries. By annotating the sites for future reference, students interact more directly with the material (rather than simply reading it), and thus become more active in the learning process.

WHO IS USING SOCIAL BOOKMARKING WITH ELL'S?

We read earlier in this chapter some ways that ESL educator Larry Ferlazzo is using social bookmarking with his ELLs. Here are some other guidelines that he developed for using this tool in the ESL classroom.

SOCIAL BOOKMARKING THAT WORKS

For social bookmarking at school with students I have very specific criteria and very specific learning purposes in mind. My criteria include:

- *The site is not blocked by my school district's content filter.*
- *Ideally, the site shows snapshots of the actual bookmarked websites and not just the address of the bookmarked site. This kind of visual support is important for English Language Learners, and I think it's useful for everybody else, too.*
- *The site allows the bookmarking of images as well as other sites, and, if there's a way for students to easily access images saved by others, then there's some kind of filter for inappropriate content.*
- *It allows the user to write notes about the site they're bookmarking.*
- *It's free, and doesn't require any download.*
- *Ideally (though this isn't a "deal-breaker") it lets others comment on what you've bookmarked.*

I have two main learning purposes in mind for students when they use a social bookmarking site:

1. *English Language Learners can identify their favorite sites from the 8,000 links on my website (http://larryferlazzo.com/english.html) and write why they like them. Other students can then access those preferences, try them out, and then comment in writing as well as directly talk to their peers about their choices. This activity can also lead to some friendly competition between students who move to computers nearby each other when they might decide to play the same language-learning games.*

2. *All students can use these sites as a tool for the higher-order of thinking activity of categorization. This can include, for example, identifying images that fit a*

specific criteria (for example, my ninth graders compiled images of Jamaican music, Jamaican history, and Jamaican nature attractions and then wrote about each one). These can also include students organizing websites or images into different categories and then having other students try to identify which ones they had in mind.

Source: Used with permission from Larry Ferlazzo. Accessed August 21, 2009, at http://larryferlazzo.edublogs.org/2008/04/16/the-best-social-bookmarking-applications-for-english-language-learners-other-students/

MAKE YOUR OWN SOCIAL BOOKMARKING PAGE

As we have seen, there are many options for social bookmarking available on the World Wide Web. Here are some options:

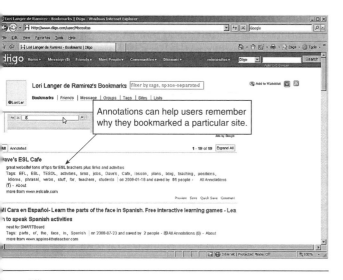

Source: Diigo.com

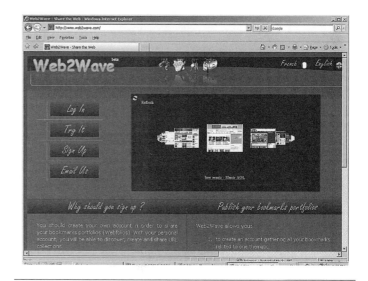

Source: Del.icio.us.com

Source: EduTaggero.com

Source: Web2Wave.com

To use Diigo in the ESL classroom, users must register for a free account (try the video on the right hand of the Diigo homepage for more details about Diigo's many applications).

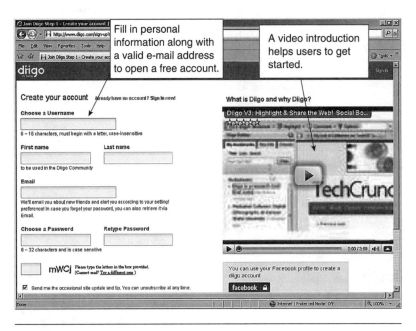

Source: Accessed May 11, 2009, at http://www.diigo.com/sign-up

After setting up your account and creating your profile, you will need to download the Diigo toolbar or applet (called the "Diigolet").

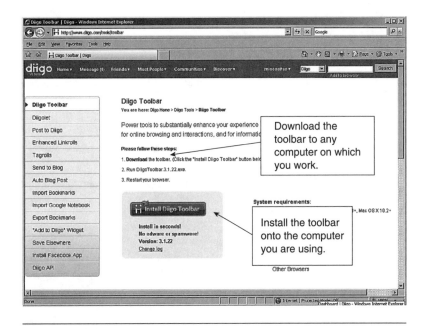

Source: Accessed May 11, 2009, at http://www.diigo.com/sign-up

Once this is done, the toolbar will appear at the top of your browser.

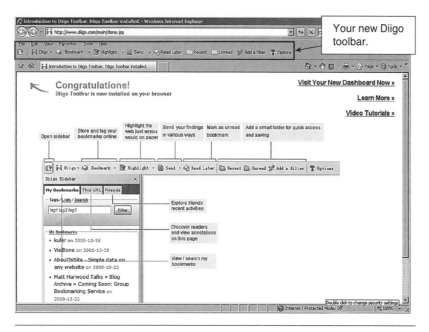

Source: Accessed May 11, 2009 at http://www.diigo.com/main/done.jsp

Now that you have the toolbar, it is as simple as clicking it and saving a particular link. It is also helpful to add comments and keywords to the description to help you to remember the site in the future and to help others to locate it as well. The resulting archive will house a list of your bookmarked sites. This archive can be further edited and arranged by topic. You can also decide to make some links public and some private. Similarly, entire archives can be made accessible to the public or not. It is easy to collect bookmarks for personal and private use while also creating a list of links for students.

There are many more features available through Diigo that can have great applicability in the ESL classroom. Once you sign up and download your toolbar, I recommend clicking through the "learn more" pages to explore how Diigo can be used as a personal research tool, a collaborative research platform, a social content site, and a knowledge-sharing community. Have fun creating and sharing your bookmarks!

● ● ●

WHERE TO FIND MORE INFORMATION ABOUT SOCIAL BOOKMARKING

SUGGESTED READINGS

Grosseck, G. (2008, December 9). Using del.icio.us in education. INFOMEDIA, The International Journal of Informatics and New media in education. Retrieved August 21, 2009, from http://www.scribd.com/doc/212002/Using-delicious-In-Education

Riddell, R. (2006, December 29). Social bookmarking makes its mark in education. eSchool News. Retrieved August 21, 2009, from http://www.eschoolnews.com/news/top-news/index.cfm?i=42069&CFID=23417953&CFTOKEN=16632444

HELPFUL WEB SITES

Education World: "Sites to See: Social Bookmarking"—Annotated links and suggestions: http://www.education-world.com/a_tech/sites/sites080.shtml

Social Bookmarking in Education—frequently asked questions: http://frequanq .blogspot.com/2005/02/social-bookmarking-in-education.html

Teacher Share: The Power of Social Bookmarking—a blog entry for teachers: http://www.education-world.com/a_tech/columnists/dyck/dyck021.shtml

Using Social Bookmarks and Del.icio.us—a video overview: http://k120nline.wm .edu/delicious/delicious.html

Virtual Worlds

Panwapa and Teen Second Life

Video connection: Prior to reading this chapter, view the online video "Getting Started in Teen Second Life" at http://www.youtube.com/watch?v=dud0Oe9n3FA

WHAT IS A VIRTUAL WORLD?

A virtual world is a computer program that simulates all of life's activities using a Web-based platform. Sometimes called "virtual reality" or "sims" (simulations), these worlds include places to visit to learn and to interact with others. They often become worlds unto themselves complete with virtual universities, concerts, museums, and other places to explore. Two such virtual worlds with applications for ESL education are Panwapa and Teen Second Life.

 PANWAPA

Panwapa was created by the makers of Sesame Street and is aimed at children ages four to seven years old. According to Panwapa.com, it is a "multimedia, global initiative that is designed to inspire and empower a new generation of children . . . to be responsible global citizens."

Source: Accessed August 21, 2009, at http://www.panwapa.com/deploy_en/print_materials/ENGLISH_panwapa_goals.pdf

> 📄 **PANWAPA**
>
> Along with interesting videos of children around the world, educational games, and other activities, Panwapa allows children to create an avatar (a cartoon identity for themselves called a "Panwapa Kid"), build their own online home, design a flag with their favorite sports, music, food and other interests, and then meet and share their information with other children on the site. The site is completely safe for young children since the sign up is anonymous (children are given a username that reflects their home country combined with a series of numbers, e.g., USA77922). Furthermore, the information that children provide on this site is guided by pull-down menus and users cannot contact each other using personal messages. Avatars are prompted to meet each other, leave calling cards, and go on quests. There are also excellent videos and other language learning activities on the site.

Source: Accessed on May 11, 2009, at http://www.panwapa.com

Figure 9.1

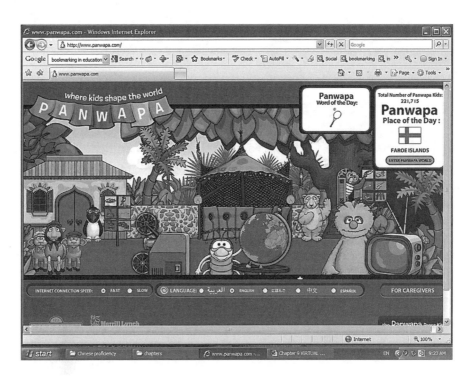

Source: Accessed on May 11, 2009, at http://www.panwapa.com

Teen Second Life is the adolescent-safe version of the adult Second Life virtual platform. According to Linden Labs' (the creators of Second Life) Web site,

📄 TEEN SECOND LIFE

Teen Second Life is an international gathering place for teens 13–17 to make friends and to play, learn and create. In Second Life, teens can create and customize a digital self called an "avatar," fly through an ever-changing 3D landscape, chat and socialize with other teens from all over the world, and build anything from skyscrapers to virtual vehicles. It's more than a videogame and much more than an Internet chat program—it's a boundless world of surprise and adventure that encourages teens to work together and use their imaginations.

Source: Accessed January 18, 2009, at http://teen.secondlife.com/whatis

Teen SL (as it is affectionately called by its users and fans) is an online world that allows teens to create an avatar that can travel through the world, talk to other residents (as you are called when you are "in world"), buy and sell virtual merchandise, go to concerts, and more. Residents go to parties, take vacations, visit friends, and go to restaurants. And lest you think that Second Life is all fun and games, universities like Harvard and Princeton have a presence "in world" on the adult version of Second Life, as do many other educational entities.

Figure 9.2

Source: Accessed January 18, 2009, at http://secondlife.com/showcase/education

While Second Life only allows users *over* the age of 18, Teen Second Life is open for kids ages 13 to 17. The Web site explains its policy regarding age restrictions on Teen Second Life:

📄 TEEN SECOND LIFE

Teen Second Life is a world for teens, created and shaped by teens . . . The only adults allowed on the mainland in Teen Second Life are Linden employees. If you are an educator and want to work with teens in Teen Second Life, there is the opportunity to buy a private island on the Teen Grid and participate, but you will not be able to leave that island and visit the Teen Grid mainland. Teens from the mainland will be able to visit your private island if/when you choose, but they will be automatically informed that there are adults present.

Source: Accessed on January 8, 2009, at https://lists.secondlife.com/cgi-bin/mailman/listinfo/educatorsandteens

Second Life has attracted criticism for being addicting and a place for escapism, but there are legitimate language-learning uses of the site. English is the *lingua franca* in Second Life, and teens can easily practice speaking with other residents. Since adults can't visit Teen Second Life, and teens can't join the adult version of Second Life, using it for English practice is easiest used for homework or "language lab" type assignments.

Components of Virtual Worlds

Panwapa's games and activities can all be accessed from the homepage. To begin building an avatar and exploring other kids' pages, a student would click on the globe icon.

Figure 9.3

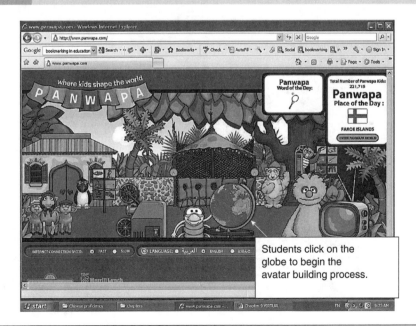

Students click on the globe to begin the avatar building process.

Source: Accessed on May 11, 2009, at http://www.panwapa.com/

In order to enter Teen Second Life (or the adult version), users first have to download the program to a computer. After providing a valid e-mail address, you choose an online name and avatar. As soon as you validate your e-mail address (by clicking on a link in an e-mail message), you can enter Second Life or Teen Second Life. Users begin in an area meant just for newcomers. Here, users find other people new to Second Life, as well as mentors who can answer questions. This welcome area is a good place to learn how to interact with the virtual environment, to practice how to walk, turn, and even fly! This area is also a good place to learn how to speak— much of which is done by typing in text, though users can also use a microphone and have one's avatar actually communicate by speaking.

Figure 9.4

An avatar explores Robert Creamer's scanner art in Teen Second Life.

An avatar explores Robert Creamer's scanner art in Teen Second Life.
Courtesy Public Library of Charlotte and Mecklenburg County, NC.

Source: Accessed January 18, 2009, at http://www.shows2go.si.edu/exhibitions/2008/05/smithsonian-and .html

Communicating in Virtual Worlds

In Panwapa, users communicate by sharing calling cards on which their country and favorite items are listed. Panwapa Kids are encouraged to go on quests to find other kids with the same taste for tacos, for example, or the same love of karate. They can even combine searches and look for kids who love cats, play the drums, and enjoy origami (all choices for their "favorites flag").

Communicating in Teen Second Life is much freer in that users can text or speak anything they want. As with chat rooms, the potential for sharing personal information exists. However, there are adult guides in Teen Second Life who monitor teen conversations. Language-learning islands and meeting places that are designed for educational purposes (like British Council Isle or Global Kids) tend to be more reliable environments for safe communication in Teen Second Life.

Figure 9.5

Source: Accessed May 15, 2009, at http://slurl.com/secondlife/Cincta/89/95/23

WHY PARTICIPATE IN VIRTUAL WORLDS WITH ELL'S?

Panwapa is a fun, easy, and safe virtual world for elementary-aged students. Once a student has built her avatar, finding and visiting other Panwapa Kids can form the basis for good compare-and-contrast activities as well as geography-based lessons. The avatar-building process in particular is an excellent source of reading and listening practice since the words for all the clothing, sports, animals, foods, and other favorites are spoken as well as appear in text. While Panwapa is particularly appropriate for English language practice, it can also be set to Arabic, Chinese, Japanese, or Spanish (with all of the activities presented in the chosen language), thus offering home language practice for bilingual classes as well.

Second Life has a large following in colleges and universities, while Teen Second Life is relatively unused in the K–12 setting. However, since it is a protected and safe online environment specifically for teens, there are many appropriate applications for Teen Second Life in the ESL classroom. When students create their own identities and travel to areas in which they can practice their English-speaking skills, it is both an exciting and enjoyable experience. As was explained in the previous section, most of the speaking experienced in Teen Second Life is actually a form of short text messages, so students will be practicing their writing skills rather than speaking. However, there is the option to use a microphone and speak, and this can also be excellent oral practice for an ESL student.

As Teen Second Life uses avatars with made-up names, ESL students feel more comfortable communicating with others without the fear of exposure in the real-world classroom. Since students can visit areas in which other ELLs are practicing English just like they are, they feel more at ease making mistakes and taking risks. Teen Second Life also gives avatars the power of using gestures to convey meaning. A simple mouse click will yield a shrug, which can help ELLs communicate lack of understanding without having to say that they don't understand. These are all means of saving face that can be very valuable to English language learners, especially at the early stages of language acquisition.

Just as the critics say, Teen Second Life can be addicting. Since there are so many worlds to visit, an infinite number of residents to meet and chat with, and even things to buy and sell, students can get lost "in world," and Teen Second Life could end up being yet another draw for the adolescent's valuable time (just like text messaging or Instant Messenger can be for some teens). It is possible, however, to see these facts as an opportunity to talk to students about time management, Internet safety, and media literacy in general. If they enjoy their Teen Second Life experience, they might want to visit after school hours. Hopefully, these visits will be to the ESL area and they will enjoy some valuable English practice there. It is important to educate students about acceptable uses of Teen Second Life so that their experiences are educational and safe as well as fun.

Quick List

Use virtual worlds for . . .

- Sharing autobiographical information via avatars
- Oral practice with virtual partners
- Pronunciation practice
- "Fantasy trips" to other countries
- Interpersonal communication practice
- Nonverbal communication practice (via avatar gestures)

HOW TO USE VIRTUAL WORLDS WITH ELL'S: SAMPLE VIRTUAL WORLDS LESSON

Before traveling "in world" with students, it is important for them to understand the ramifications of visiting virtual worlds. Here is an example of an activity that ELLs can enjoy without ever signing on to Teen Second Life.

Have students read the report below.

Children Learn Social Skills in Web Worlds

New research carried out by the BBC suggests that children aged 6–12 can learn important social skills in virtual worlds. The BBC website says: "Virtual worlds can be valuable places where children rehearse what they will do in real life." The study's lead researcher, Professor David Gauntlett, stated that children interacting with others online and exploring web worlds was better for kids than passive pastimes like watching TV. He said the children adopted different roles when they ventured through the virtual world; some were explorers, others were social climbers, while others were fighters or collectors. Professor Gauntlett indicated that the virtual world was a safe place for children to rehearse real-life situations without the negative or painful consequences of the real world.

The BBC's research was carried out using its own Children's BBC online world called *Adventure Rock*. In it, children have to explore, create things and ask questions as they go deeper into the game. It is a closed world where children's avatars cannot meet or communicate. Kids can share tips and hints for other users on a message board, which is controlled and edited by BBC staff. There are none of the chat rooms or discussion boards normally found in virtual worlds like Second Life. The emphasis is on safety for kids in an online environment without advertising and sales gimmicks. Researchers also asked parents about their feelings towards their children spending time in *Adventure Rock*. The findings were presented at the Conference on Virtual Worlds for Children on 23 May 2008.

Source: Breaking News English. Accessed August 21, 2009, at http://www.breakingnewsenglish.com/0805/080524-social_skills.html

In order to get students to think critically about the information they read in the previous article, initiate discussions based on the following questions and prompts:

Warm-Ups

1. **Online Kids:** How many children go on line each day? Who wants and does not want kids to be online? With your partners, discuss how you think the following people feel about children being online: children, parents, teachers, advertising executives, psychologists.

2. **Social Skills:** Where best can children learn social skills? Rank the items below: 10 = "an unbeatable place to learn social skills;" 1 = "a great way to produce a social misfit." Compare your answers with your partners.

Table 9.1

_____ school	_____ shopping malls
_____ parks and playgrounds	_____ clubs
_____ television	_____ books
_____ the home	_____ online virtual worlds

3. **Virtual Reality:** Spend one minute writing down all of the different words you associate with the term _virtual reality._ Share your words with your partners and talk about them. Together, put the words into different categories.

Prereading/Listening

1. **True/False:** Look at the article's headline, and guess whether these sentences are true (T) or false (F):

   ___ Kids learn better social skills online than they do in the real world.

   ___ Kids can rehearse and practice social skills when they're online.

   ___ Being online in a virtual world is not as good for kids as watching TV.

   ___ The virtual world teaches kids how to punch and fight.

   ___ The research was done using a BBC site especially for children.

   ___ Kids took part in online discussions and chat just like in the real world.

   ___ The BBC site is set to make a lot of money from commercials and ads.

   ___ The BBC asked parents for their feelings on their kids being online.

2. **Synonym Match:** Match the following synonyms from the article:

Table 9.2

1.	virtual	a.	conducted
2.	rehearse	b.	tricks
3.	ventured	c.	expressed
4.	indicated	d.	imitation
5.	consequences	e.	journeyed
6.	carried out	f.	stress
7.	avatars	g.	conclusions
8.	emphasis	h.	results
9.	gimmicks	i.	alias icon
10.	findings	j.	practice

After Reading/Listening

1. **Word Search:** Look in your dictionaries or computer to find other meanings, information, and synonyms for the words *virtual* and *world.*
   - Share your findings with your partners.
   - Make questions using the words you found.
   - Ask your partner or group your questions.

2. **Article Questions:** Look back at the article and write down some questions you would like to ask the class about the text.
   - Share your questions with other classmates or groups.
   - Ask your partner or group your questions.

3. **Vocabulary:** Circle any words you do not understand. In groups, pool unknown words, and use dictionaries to find their meanings.

Children's Internet Discussion

Student A's Questions (Do not show these to Student B)

a. What did you think when you read the headline?

b. What springs to mind when you hear the term *virtual world*?

c. What do your grandparents think of virtual worlds?

d. Is it a good idea to let six- and seven-year-olds roam around in virtual worlds?

e. How possible is it for children to learn social skills in an Internet game?

f. What dangers are there for young children while online?

g. Do you think wandering around in a virtual world in an online game is better than watching television?

h. Where did you learn most of your social skills, and what are they?

i. Do you think children should rehearse real-life situations or experience them for real (together with the pain)?

j. Are you an explorer, a social climber, a fighter, or a collector?

Student B's Questions (Do not show these to Student A)

a. Did you like reading this article?

b. Would you like to venture into the BBC's Adventure Rock world?

c. Do you think children learn more by creating things and exploring in the real world?

d. Do you have an avatar? What kind of avatar would you like?

e. Do you think children should be allowed to communicate with other users of their virtual world?

f. What do you know about other virtual worlds, like Second Life?

g. Do you think advertisers should be allowed into virtual worlds for kids?

h. How would you feel about your six-year-old spending time online?

i. What questions would you like to ask Professor David Gauntlett?

j. Did you like this discussion?

Homework

1. **Internet:** Search the Internet and find out more about *Adventure Rock*. Share what you discover with your partners in the next lesson.

2. **Virtual Worlds:** Make a poster about the virtual worlds that exist on the Internet. Show your work to your classmates in the next lesson. Did you all have similar things?

3. **Concerned Parent:** Write a magazine article about the good and bad things about kids entering virtual worlds. Include imaginary interviews with a six-year-old who loves being online and his concerned parents. Include questions about rehearsing real-life situations. Read what you wrote to your classmates in the next lesson. Write down any new words and expressions you hear from your partners.

4. **Letter:** Write a letter to Professor David Gauntlett. Ask him three questions about his research and virtual worlds. Give him three pieces of advice on what he should tell game makers to keep children safe. Read your letter to your partners in your next lesson. Your partners will answer your questions.

5. **Diary/Journal:** You are a six-year-old. Write your diary entry about one day in your life online in your virtual world. Include your thoughts on the real world. Which is better? Read your entry to your classmates in the next lesson.

Source: This lesson was created by Sean Banville from www.BreakingNewsEnglish.com. The accompanying mp3 file can be found at http://www.breakingnewsenglish.com/0805/080524-social_skills.html

Sample Virtual Worlds Lesson: Standards Correlations

Students read or listen to a news report about virtual worlds for children.		
21st-Century Skills	**TESOL Standards**	**TESOL Tech Standards**
• Core Subjects and 21st-Century Themes • Media Literacy • Information Literacy	• Goal 2, Standard 2: Students use English to obtain, process, construct, and provide subject-matter information in spoken and written forms. • Goal 2, Standard 3: Students will use appropriate learning strategies to construct and apply academic knowledge.	• n/a

Students discuss and question the importance and relevance of virtual worlds in their lives.		
21st-Century Skills	**TESOL Standards**	**TESOL Tech Standards**
• Critical Thinking and Problem-Solving Skills • Communication and Collaboration Skills • Media Literacy • Information Literacy	• Goal 2, Standard 1: Students will use English to interact in the classroom. • Goal 2, Standard 2: Students use English to obtain, process, construct, and provide subject-matter information in spoken and written forms. • Goal 3, Standard 1: Students will use the appropriate language variety, register, and genre according to audience, purpose, and setting.	• Goal 3: Students use technology-based tools as aids in the development of their language-learning competence as part of formal instruction and for further learning.

Students search for and define new vocabulary words and structures through reading and writing about the topic of virtual worlds.

21st-Century Skills	TESOL Standards	TESOL Tech Standards
• Critical Thinking and Problem-Solving Skills • Core Subjects and 21st-Century Themes	• Goal 2, Standard 2: Students use English to obtain, process, construct, and provide subject-matter information in spoken and written forms. • Goal 2, Standard 3: Students will use appropriate learning strategies to construct and apply academic knowledge.	• Goal 3: Students use technology-based tools as aids in the development of their language-learning competence as part of formal instruction and for further learning.

Safety Tips for Students "In World"

Teens visiting the "Teen Grid" (Teen Second Life) would do well to abide by the following guidelines:

- **Stay Anonymous.** Don't ever tell anyone online your real full name, your parents' names, your home address, your school name or location, your phone or cell phone numbers, social security or credit card numbers, and do not post anything that shows what you look like, such as a photo, video, or Webcam link. If someone asks you for this info, don't give it to them, and report the incident at "Report Abuse" on the Help Menu.

- **Keep Your Password to Yourself.** Friends don't ask friends to share passwords. If you give your password to someone, they will have access to all of your account information and your inventory items. Not to mention, you'll be held responsible for anything they do while using your account. Linden Lab employees will never ask you for your password.

- **Don't Respond to Nasty Comments or Actions.** If a mean or inappropriate comment or action is directed at you, the best thing to do is ignore it and report it at "Report Abuse" on the Help Menu. You can use the "Mute" button on a resident's profile window to ignore their chat. You can also "Ban" them from visiting land that you purchased.

- **Trust Your Instincts.** If someone makes you feel uncomfortable or threatened, use the Mute button on their profile window and report them at "Report Abuse" on the Help Menu. If you ever get really scared, you should log off immediately. Don't worry about seeming rude. If someone is making you feel uncomfortable, they're the ones being rude. Remember, in Second Life the exit is only a click away.

- **Keep Your Parents in the Loop About Your Second Life.** Tell your parents about your Second Life friends and your favorite things to do in world. Show them around every now and then. Don't be afraid to ask for their help when you need it.

(Continued)

(Continued)

- **Beware of Online Advice Givers.** The best place to seek advice for really serious issues like depression, health problems, or trouble at home or at school is a trusted adult offline. Beware of anyone online who claims to be a counselor or therapist wanting to help you with these types of issues. They may not really have your best interests in mind.

- **If It Sounds Too Good to Be True, It Probably Is.** Don't believe anyone in Teen Second Life who tells you they are a famous celebrity. You may really want it to be true, but it's best to be skeptical of these claims, especially if they ask for your password or for personal information. The same goes for anyone who tells you they are a modeling agent, music agent, or movie agent in real life.

- **Never Meet Offline.** Teen Second Life friendships should stay in game. Never meet any of your Teen Second Life friends offline unless you are attending an official Linden Lab gathering with your parents.

Source: Accessed January 18, 2009, at http://teen.secondlife.com/parents/safety

WHEN TO VISIT VIRTUAL WORLDS WITH ELL'S

There are specific age requirements for Teen Second Life that will dictate when to use this Web 2.0 technology with ELLs. Social bookmarking sites can be used at all grades with English Language learners.

Grades K–5

Students can sign on to Panwapa and create their own avatar. The avatar creation process consists of several screens that each deals with a different aspect of the avatar's physical identity: body color, eyes and mouth, hair, clothes, headwear, and footwear. This is a great connection to vocabulary of physical description and clothing.

Students at this age *cannot* use Teen Second Life.

Grades 6–8

Starting at Age 13, students in middle school can use Teen Second Life. Teachers might ask students to create an avatar and talk with another resident about a simple topic like the school day, hobbies, or favorite music. Students can take a screen shot of the interaction and report back to the class about the conversation. They can also read news articles about online virtual worlds and set up a debate on the advantages and disadvantages of spending time in world.

Grades 9–12

Older students can participate in Teen Second Life by setting up conferences and presentations for other residents in world. Students who are 18 and over can graduate to the adult version of Second Life and visit the

English Learning World, university areas (like Princeton and Harvard), and other areas that involve the students in practicing their academic or social English.

WHO IS VISITING VIRTUAL WORLDS WITH ELL'S?

Ellen Clegg is Academic Director for ELS Language Centers in San Antonio, Texas. Ellen shares the following story about using Second Life with her older students. It is interesting to read about her experiences with the program and learn how she came to love the environment for its applications in the ESL classroom. (Note: In the real world, she can be reached at eclegg@els.edu and, in Second Life, she can be IMed as Rhonwen Beresford.)

GET A SECOND LIFE!

Second Life (SL) is an immersive, interactive learning environment. This is not the normal perception, but it is the reality. For those who've never done SL it's perceived as a game. But for those who have some experience with the virtual world, SL is a rich tool for language learning.

Second Life is a 3-dimensional virtual world in which your avatar (gamer talk for the figure that represents you) is able to move about, explore numerous and varied islands or sims (short for simulations), communicate in text or voice chat, shop for personal items, create objects, participate in role playing games, and meet people from all over the world.

My curiosity about virtual worlds and SL was piqued when I read some articles about SL in the business section of our local paper. I went to the website, but was hesitant about signing up, because I didn't quite understand what Second Life was. After several weeks, I got brave enough to set up a free account. I think it was even a few more weeks before I went through the official Second Life orientation—and that was scary! I landed in a hilly area with other new avatars flying in around me. There were mentors there to talk to, but I didn't even know what to ask. I walked through the orientation/training. Orientation ended up in a freebie mall, but I still didn't understand how to buy things—even free things. Orientation was useful, but I still didn't feel completely comfortable in SL.

After orientation, I started wandering around. My avatar (Rhonwen Beresford) was too shy at first to talk to anyone else. The first time I talked to someone "in world," I had an actual physical fear/anxiety response—my real life body became very tense. The idea that there was someone, a real person somewhere in the world on the other side of the avatar I was speaking with, was very disorienting. I got through it, had my first brief conversation—and lived in Second Life (and real life) to tell about it. What I also learned was that more experienced SL residents (yes, that's what they are called) love to help a "newbie." I was hooked—meeting people in this new environment was fun and engaging.

I started exploring and found all sorts of visually exciting sims: medieval role play, elf homes, modern shopping malls, fantasy gardens, live music venues, recreations of historical environments (60's San Francisco), literary environments (Nathaniel Hawthorne's house and Macbeth's castle), libraries in all languages, international sims (Casablanca and Paris), and areas devoted to English language learning.

After I'd been in world for about three months, I had acquired some movement control, seen some stimulating places, and talked to enough interesting people to realize that this was an invaluable learning tool. As I wandered through SL and explored different sims, I saw that it was a language-rich environment dense with interactive ways of using English:

- *Signage is everywhere*
- *Information is often conveyed in note cards*
- *Text chat is more prevalent than voice chat*
- *All objects have information/directions attached*
- *There are lush, detailed visuals supported by text descriptions*

Some ESL teachers are already using SL for instruction—they are holding classes in world (inside Second Life) at Second Life English and English Village. Rather than teaching in world, my concept is to use SL as an adjunct to class—a source of the realia that is so hard for teachers to drag into the classroom or to get students out of the classroom to experience.

The first educational information I found about SL was in the Second Life Educators Listserve which can be subscribed to through the SL website (https://lists .secondlife.com/cgi-bin/mailman/listinfo/educators). This contains invaluable information (mostly for college level) and intriguing discussions about virtual worlds and their educational uses. Through this I have found new places to visit and learned how people in other fields are using Second Life.

Through Second Life, I've met a Brazilian computer programmer, a Swedish musician (you should hear him play his virtual cello!), teachers actively using SL for ESL, a French teacher, several librarians (library science is big in SL), and a university instructor from Dublin. I've also reconnected with one of our former Academic Directors who now teaches in Second Life for Language Lab.

While Second Life offers exciting possibilities for ESL instruction, there are at this time some hurdles. Although possible to do SL on an ordinary run-of-the-mill office computer, the visuals and load time really work best on a computer with a high-end graphics card and LOTS of memory (exact specs are on the SL website). Another issue, I've run into is resistance from students. SL is often perceived as a game, so our adult, more serious students fear that they will not learn anything from using it. The last major hurdle is the amount of time it takes to learn Second Life. I've found that many educators are working on ways to shorten the learning curve through cheat sheets and clearer orientations.

Why is Second Life worth so much trouble? The immersiveness of the SL experience leads people to feel they have physically done what they have experienced, thereby reinforcing retention. Educators are seeing that this interactive quality of SL can be an invaluable learning tool. Giving students a chance to create or re-create themselves produces a more engaged learner. While actually teaching in world seems too restricted/involved for the academic bound students in the intensive language program I direct, I feel that it could be put to great use as an ancillary to the in-class experience—a way to get students out of the classroom and exploring how to use their language skills in a "real" environment.

While still in the early adopter phase, virtual worlds have a lot of potential for education. I encourage you to experiment with them for yourself and I look forward to meeting you in world!

Source: Used with permission from Ellen Clegg. Personal correspondence, 2009.

JOIN THE VIRTUAL WORLD

For young children, Panwapa or Panfu are two excellent—and safe—virtual worlds. Two of the most popular virtual worlds online for older students are Teen Second Life (ages 13–17) and Second Life (ages 18+).

Source: Teen.SecondLife.com

Source: SecondLife.com

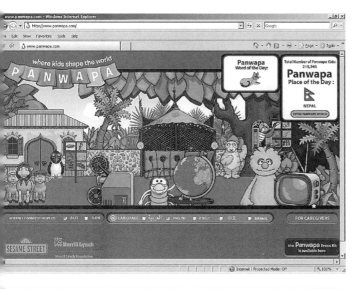

Source: Panwapa.com

Source: Panfu.com

To begin creating an avatar (or a "kid" as they are called) in Panwapa, students first establish a username and password.

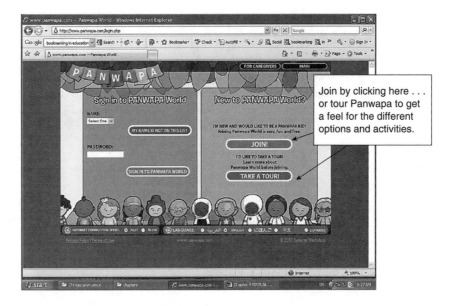

Children will then be walked through the process of developing their kid.

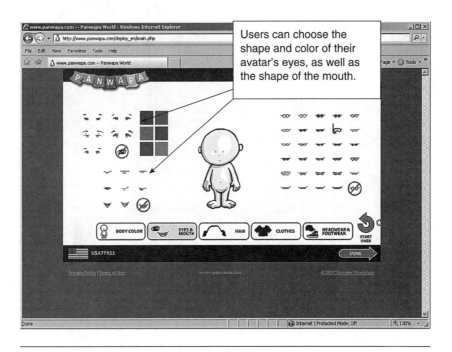

Source: Accessed May 11, 2009, at http://www.panwapa.com/login.php

After the "kid" is complete, students will build a virtual home and design a flag with six of their favorites (food, animals, sports, musical instruments, activities, and crafts).

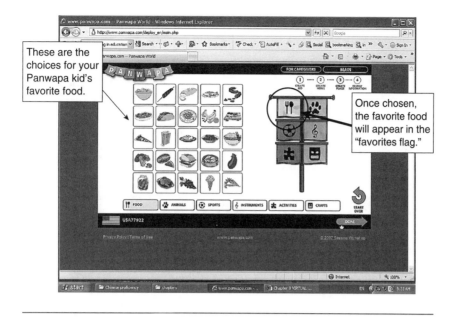

Source: Accessed May 11, 2009, at http://www.panwapa.com/deploy_en/main.php

After designing a Panwapa kid, home, and flag, students will be able to travel around Panwapa Island to meet other kids and trade Panwapa cards.

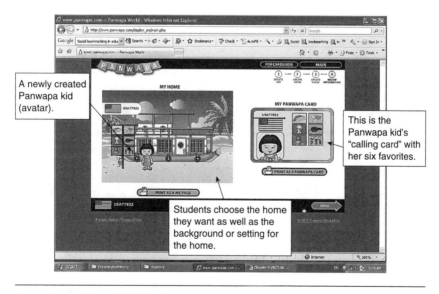

Source: Accessed May 11, 2009, at http://www.panwapa.com/deploy_en/main.php

Students can also visit other parts of the world to meet other Panwapa kids.

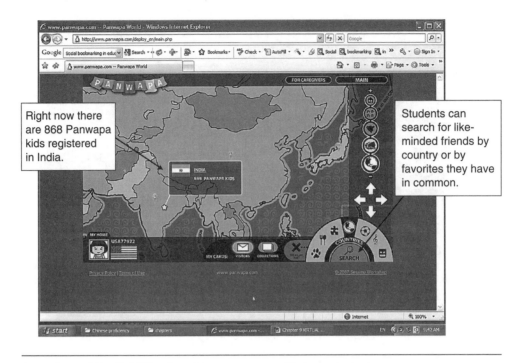

Right now there are 868 Panwapa kids registered in India.

Students can search for like-minded friends by country or by favorites they have in common.

Source: Accessed May 11, 2009, at http://www.panwapa.com/deploy_en/main.php

If you are interested in exploring Teen Second Life for use with your students, it would be helpful to start by downloading and signing on to the adult version of Second Life so that you can understand the environment and ways in which an avatar interacts with others. Create an avatar for yourself and start learning how to move, talk, and travel.

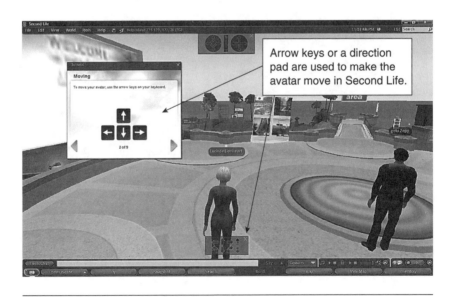

Arrow keys or a direction pad are used to make the avatar move in Second Life.

Source: Accessed on January 18, 2009, at Second Life.com

Once you learn how to navigate the virtual world, you can visit different islands and talk to residents there. It is also recommended that you explore the many educational projects and activities online, as well as lectures, classes, and opportunities for avatars to practice English while in world.

WHERE TO FIND MORE INFORMATION ABOUT VIRTUAL WORLDS

SUGGESTED READINGS

Baere, K. (2008). ESL in Second Life. *About.com.* Retrieved August 21, 2009, from http://esl.about.com/od/esleflteachingtechnique/a/l-slife.htm

Briggs, L. (2007, August). The teen grid: Bringing your school into Second Life. *T.H.E. Journal—Transforming Education Through Technology.* Retrieved August 21, 2009, from http://www.thejournal.com/articles/21101

Parker, Q. (2007, April 6). A second look at school life. *Guardian.* Retrieved August 21, 2009, from http://www.guardian.co.uk/education/2007/apr/06/schools.uk

Sesame Workshop. (2008). *Six new characters foster global citizenship from a floating island: Panwapa helps children gain empathy for others while encouraging a broader international perspective.* Retrieved August 21, 2009, from http://www.sesameworkshop.org/initiatives/respect/panwapa

Sesame Workshop. (2008). *Panwapa press kit: Questions and answers with international advisors.* Retrieved August 21, 2009, from http://archive.sesameworkshop.org/aboutus/pressroom/presskits/panwapa/qa-advisor.php

HELPFUL WEB SITES

English Village ESL in Second Life—a video of English Village, a 3D simulation in Second Life for language teachers and learners: http://www.teachertube.com/view_video.php?viewkey=a8d5fdb372271e980da6

Second Life English Blog—a detailed blog with links, videos, and explanations about the Second Life English community: http://esl-secondlife.blogspot.com

Second Life Resources—a long list of Second Life links: http://sleducation.wikispaces.com/secondliferesources

Index